Smart Thinking for Crazy Times

IAN MITROFF

SMART THINKING for Crazy Times

The Art of Solving the Right Problems

Berrett-Koehler Publishers, Inc.
San Francisco

Berrett-Koehler Publishers, Inc.
450 Sansome Street, Suite 1200
San Francisco, CA 94111-3320
Tel: (415) 288-0260 Fax: (415) 362-2512

Ordering Information

Individual sales. Berrett-Koehler publications are available through most bookstores. They can also be ordered direct from Berrett-Koehler at the address above.

Quantity sales. Special discounts are available on quantity purchases by corporations, associations, and others. For details, contact the "Special Sales Department" at the Berrett-Koehler address above.

Orders for college textbook/course adoption use. Please contact Berrett-Koehler Publishers at the address above.

Orders by U.S. trade bookstores and wholesalers. Please contact Publishers Group West, 4065 Hollis Street, Box 8843, Emeryville, CA 94662. Tel: (510) 658-3453; 1-800-788-3123. Fax: (510) 658-1834.

Printed in the United States of America

 Printed on acid-free and recycled paper that is composed of 50% recovered fiber, including 10% postconsumer waste.

Library of Congress Cataloging-in-Publication Data

Mitroff, Ian I.
    Smart thinking for crazy times: the art of solving the right problems / Ian Mitroff.—1st ed.
       p. cm.
    Includes bibliographical references and index.
    ISBN 1-57675-020-5 (alk. paper)
    1. Problem solving. 2. Critical thinking. 3. Creative thinking.
I. Title.
BF449.M6   1997
153.4'3—dc21   97-43556
                                               CIP

First Edition
05 04 03 02 01 00 99 98   10 9 8 7 6 5 4 3 2 1

Copyediting: Mary Lou Sumberg
Proofreading: PeopleSpeak
Interior design and production: Joel Friedlander, Marin Bookworks
Indexing: Directions Unlimited
Jacket: Sue Malikowski

This book is dedicated to
the memory of my brother, Michael.

When asked what single event was most helpful in developing the theory of relativity, Albert Einstein is reported to have answered, "Figuring out how to think about the problem."

—Richard Saul Wurman,
Information Anxiety

Contents

Preface

In today's world, the margin for error has all but vanished. Increasingly, it is necessary to get problems right the first time out of the box, or there will be no second time. One false move, one inappropriate or wrong statement, one gaff is almost enough to destroy an organization, seriously tarnish its reputation, alienate countless parties, or make it an easy target for critics. The danger lies not only in *picking* the wrong problems on which to spend limited energies—solving the wrong problems precisely—but far worse, in *creating* more serious problems as a result.

Why do individuals, organizations, and even whole societies repeatedly get trapped into solving the wrong problems precisely, and how can we break out of this trap? Why do some individuals and organizations consistently go down the wrong paths, and how can we choose the right ones? Once we have started down the wrong path, how can we come to know it, stop in our tracks, and reverse our steps? Finally, how can the process of focusing on the right problems be made easier? These questions are the challenges addressed by this book.

Problems versus Exercises

It may be a cliché to say that in today's world we face issues of unparalleled complexity. It may also be a cliché to say that our educational system is not preparing students for the high-level, creative-thinking skills they require. But clichés or not, we must acknowledge that for the most part our educational system, from top to bottom, mainly *trains* students to tackle prepackaged, canned exercises, instead of *educating* them to confront complex problems. And canned exercises are not merely for students but, all too often for instructors, general citizens, and organizations as well.

Why does our educational system have this focus? As John Dewey so eloquently put it long ago, Western society is generally obsessed with the "quest for certainty."[1] As a method of instruction, let alone as a model of knowledge, canned exercises would not have persisted for so long if they did not serve a fundamental social need: the reduction of anxiety brought on by a world of extreme uncertainty.

Many business books compound this problem; they mislead students and practitioners alike by assuming that the problems of an organization are obvious and have a single solution, such as downsizing, Total Quality Management (TQM), or reengineering. As a result, business books actually contribute to the error of solving the wrong problems precisely.

Real-world problems, on the other hand, must be correctly formulated before they can be solved. This book introduces readers to the *art of formulating problems, not solving canned exercises*. It teaches how to confront uncertainty, not flee from it. It teaches one of the most important and vital of all skills: critical thinking, or what I call smart thinking.

Smart Thinking

While exhortations abound constantly about the need for critical thinking, books on how to actually achieve it with real problems are in short supply. This book fills that gap. It is for managers, executives, and policy makers, as well as citizens in all walks of life; it is for people who need to cut through the confusion and focus their efforts on identifying and solving the right problems—in short, people who need to think critically.

This book is based on my thirty years of consultation, research, seminars, and teaching with audiences and organizations of all kinds. Using concrete examples from the world of business and all walks of life, it teaches readers how to identify and avoid the most common errors that prevent individuals and organizations from solving the right problems. It shows how to formulate important problems from multiple perspectives, which contributes to expanding options and helps to avoid solving the wrong problems precisely.

Part one of this book goes into great detail about critical thinking. It previews the five common errors that individuals and organizations make in formulating problems and how to avoid them. Part two devotes one chapter to each of the five errors and the strategies for avoiding them. Building on the concepts discussed in part two, part three examines how organizations can create and manage teams that will be more likely to formulate problems correctly.

Smart Thinking for Crazy Times is not another business book about managerial problem solving. It is concerned with how the rarest of all human commodities—wisdom—can be better infused into the lives of individuals and institutions. Increasingly, the fate of the United States, as well as of every society on the face of the planet, depends less and less on those who can solve canned problems and more and more on leaders—critical or smart thinkers in the best sense of the term—who can define, and then redefine, the hellishly difficult problems facing humankind.

The ability to spot the right problems and then formulate them correctly is the critical skill that all workers, managers, and top executives must possess if they are to compete successfully in the twenty-first century. Organizations that know how to think critically will dominate. Individuals who know how to think critically will make better and wiser decisions in their lives.

—Ian Mitroff,
December 1997

Acknowledgments

First and foremost, I want to thank my wife, Donna, who encouraged me to write this book. She read the entire manuscript through the various stages of its preparation and offered valuable criticism and, most of all, encouragement. For over thirty-four years, she has helped me to formulate wise solutions to problems, and together we have learned how to reformulate many of our most vexing problems.

I am indebted to the following individuals for providing me with invaluable ideas and constant support: Vince Barabba, Gerald Gordon, Maxene Johnston, Jean Lipman-Blumen, Irv Margol, Richard O. Mason, Kurt Motamedi, Stephen Toulmin, Niraj Verma, and Gerald Zaltman. Daniel Landau helped with research on various phases of the project.

I also want to single out my daughter, Dana, who is a constant source of inspiration and who continually offered helpful ideas throughout the preparation of the manuscript.

I am greatly indebted to Steve Piersanti, the publisher of Berrett-Koehler, who not only nourished the manuscript throughout its various stages but helped with the basic organization and statement of the underlying ideas. In this same vein, I also wish to thank Charles T. Dorris, who helped with the editing of the manuscript.

Lastly, I especially wish to acknowledge the constant friendship and invaluable support of Warren Bennis. Warren read and offered valuable criticisms on the various drafts of the book. He is one of the wisest persons I know when it comes to formulating problems. He is the best friend one could have.

The Foundation for Smart Thinking

PART ONE

Part one provides the building blocks for understanding what critical thinking is and for learning how to formulate problems correctly.

Chapter 1 uses a case study to illustrate the error of solving the wrong problem precisely. It discusses some of the concepts behind critical thinking, such as the difference between an exercise and a problem; asks some questions that challenge taken-for-granted assumptions; and lays out the four steps of the problem-solving process.

Chapter 2 introduces the following five basic categories of solving the wrong problem precisely:

1. Picking the wrong stakeholders.

2. Selecting too narrow a set of options.

3. Phrasing a problem incorrectly.

4. Setting the boundaries/scope of a problem too narrowly.

5. Failing to think systemically.

It also introduces strategies for avoiding these errors and, thus, ways to formulate problems correctly.

CHAPTER 1

The Critical Need for Critical Thinking

After weighing various schemes [for fighting the 1992 Gulf War] for more than four hours, I realized I'd asked the question the wrong way.

—General H. Norman Schwartzkopf,
It Doesn't Take a Hero

THIS IS AN UNCONVENTIONAL BOOK ABOUT MANAGEMENT. It is about why we so often fail to make the right decisions, let alone wise ones. Even more, it is about how we can learn the art of making wise decisions.

Breaking the Tyranny of Fads

The dictionary defines a *fad* as a "craze or fashion that is taken up with great enthusiasm for a brief period of time." Even more interesting and provocative, the dictionary hypothesizes that *fiddle-faddle* is the most likely origin of the word fad. In turn, fiddle-faddle is defined as "nonsense." If fiddle-faddle is therefore the ultimate meaning of fad, then a fad is literally "the adoption of nonsense."

It is precisely because management is not an exact science, and perhaps never will be—at least not in its entirety—that it is prone to fads. The tendency to leap from one fad to the next, to adopt the latest with the same zeal and enthusiasm as previous fads were adopted and to abandon each in succession and as quickly as the next appears is responsible for much of the cynicism and despair in today's organizations. In more than one organization with which my colleagues and I have worked, the employees play the following game: the person or persons who come closest to guessing the name of next year's management craze are the winners of a sizable pool of money! If fads fool anyone, it is those at the top who push them, not those at the bottom and in the middle who are forced to implement and suffer them.

This is not to say that Total Quality Management, reengineering, downsizing, and other management programs are totally worthless. They are worthless only if they are conceived of as total cure-alls, and especially if they are jettisoned as soon as the next cure-all appears on the horizon. In a sense, it does not really matter which particular program management adopts as long as it sticks to it consistently for at least five to seven years and, further, as long as the program is done critically and system wide. Does this mean that programs should never be modified or abandoned? No. It means that the decisions about continuation or abandonment of important programs need to be made on the basis of critical thinking and, most of all, wisdom.

Smart Thinking: The Only True and Lasting Competitive Edge

As far as I know, there is only one true and consistent way of not getting caught in fads: the constant exercise of critical or smart thinking. The need for smart thinking has never been greater. While smart thinking has never been a luxury, it is an absolute necessity in today's world.

Those who are adept at smart thinking know how to cut through complex issues, ask the right questions, and solve the right problems. The ability to spot the right problems, frame them correctly, and implement appropriate solutions to them is the true competitive edge that will separate the successful individuals, organizations, and societies from the also-rans.

There is a wise saying that "the person who controls the definition of a problem controls its solution." Equally wise are these observations: "a problem well put is half solved"; "the first definition of an important problem is almost always wrong"; and "never trust a single definition of an important problem."

If the exercise of critical thinking is the ultimate competitive advantage, then its absence often leads to major crises. As a result, this book is interested in both positive and negative examples of critical thinking. In the negative cases, we examine what went wrong and why. In the positive cases, we examine why some individuals and organizations have a talent for avoiding costly errors and crises. In both cases, our aim is to extract basic lessons so that both individuals and organizations can learn to think smarter and more wisely.

The positive effects of critical thinking will be better appreciated after we have examined what happens when such thinking is absent. Let us start, therefore, with an example of what can happen when an organization with exemplary goals fails to think critically and therefore creates a major crisis for itself.

A Textbook Case of Solving the Wrong Problem Precisely

For sixteen years, the Make-A-Wish Foundation has granted the wishes of terminally ill children. In the process, it has become one of the most respected charities worldwide. Recently, however, it was criticized severely for

> [helping to arrange] what a teenager suffering from a brain tumor wanted most: to shoot a Kodiak bear in Alaska.

> But, [the Make-A-Wish Foundation] didn't blink. It turned to Safari Club International, which collected donations, including $4,000, airline tickets, a Weatherby .340-magnum rifle, binoculars, hunting clothing, an outfitter, and a taxidermist.

Now, the program that has provided thousands of families with joyful memories to help ease the depression of losing a child is on the hit list of virtually every animal-rights group in the nation.[1]

The decision to grant the teenager's wish is a tragic, but classic, example of the failure to think critically. The result is almost always the same: solving the wrong problem.

If we assume that the basic problem is how to grant the wish and that Safari Club International is the most effective means available to solve it, then the combined decision to grant the wish and to use Safari Club International is a premiere example of *solving the wrong problem precisely and in the most efficient way possible.* That is, if we grant that Safari Club International is the "most effective means available" of solving the initial problem of "how to grant the teenager's wish," then Safari Club International is the "best" solution. This is a prime example of muddled thinking because, as we will show in chapter 2, the assumptions that underlay the formulation of the problem were not examined critically.

Formulating Problems and Solutions

A joke about a not-too-bright farmer and an equally dim-witted agricultural extension agent is useful for understanding the importance of formulating a problem correctly.

A farmer ordered a dozen chicks from a catalogue. He planted them head first in the ground and watered them thoroughly. When the chicks failed to sprout, he ordered another dozen. This time he planted them feet first and watered them as before. When they also failed to sprout, he ordered still another dozen and froze them in his freezer. He planted these as before and watered them. When these also failed to grow, he wired his local agricultural extension agent asking for help. He shortly received a letter saying that the agent was as puzzled as the farmer, but that he would be glad to help if he could. If the farmer would merely send the agent a sample of his soil, he would be willing to analyze it for its acidity.

To put it mildly, this joke is another illustration of *solving the wrong problem precisely.* The farmer defined the problem as a "planting problem," that is, which method of planting chicks was best? The agricultural extension agent, on the other hand, defined the problem as a "soil acidity" problem; that is, which level of soil acidity was best for growing chicks?

This joke is also an illustration of a deeper issue: problems do not drop preformulated from the heavens. Real problems, unlike the typical exercises found at the end of the vast majority of textbooks, are not given to us. They are extracted, often with great difficulty, from messy and complex situations. Thus, before we can *solve* a problem, we must first *formulate* it. And before we can formulate a problem, we must know the difference between the types of problems that we have been taught to solve in school (which I call exercises) and real human problems.

Most textbooks, whether elementary or advanced, convey the false impression that unless something can be stated clearly and unambiguously in one and only one way, it is not a problem worthy of consideration. This condition applies, if at all, only to a very limited class of problems—not to important ones. All problems worthy of the name have more than one way of being stated. Indeed, we may say that something is a problem *if and only if* there is more than one way of stating it!

Since problems, unlike exercises, have more than one way of being stated, or formulated, they also have more than one solution. For example, in the case of the Make-A-Wish Foundation, if the problem had been stated as how to grant the wish of a child without violating ethical constraints, a different solution might have been found. The foundation could have redefined the notion of "shooting a bear" to mean "shooting a picture of a bear," not literally taking its life. Then the problem would have been finding the most effective way of getting the child to Alaska and helping the child to take a picture of the animal.

Exercises, on the other hand, are both *bounded* and *structured*. By bounded, I mean that the potential solutions are limited in number. By structured, I mean that the exercise is phrased unambiguously in the precise language of algebra. Thus, "$x + 6 = 11$; find x" is not a problem. It is an exercise because it is preformulated and given, and there is only one solution, $x = 5$.

In bounded and structured exercises, the various potential solutions are either given or can be discovered with relative ease. In general, this is not true of problems. A central feature of most problems is the difficulty of discovering the various potential solutions, which have to be generated by the problem solver. For example, questions of how to end the animosity and hatred in the Middle East or of how to make American business more ethical and more productive at the same time are problems in the truest sense of the word, because there is more than one way of formulating each of them. And as a result, there is more than one solution.

One Fundamental Flaw

All serious errors of management can be traced to one fundamental flaw, solving the wrong problem precisely, or muddled thinking. The majority of books on management contribute to and maintain this flaw because they imply that managers already know what their important problems are, for example, how to downsize in the most efficient way, how to improve chances for success in the global economy, how to instill the correct TQM or reengineering approach, how to design the right reward system, and so on. In each case, the unstated assumptions are that the essential problem the organization is facing is downsizing, global competitiveness, or whatever it may be. While the assumptions may be correct, they are so crucial to formulating the problem correctly that they deserve to be challenged in the strongest possible way by asking tough questions.

All serious errors of management can be traced to one fundamental flaw: solving the wrong problem precisely, or muddled thinking.

Tough Questions That Challenge Assumptions

The ability to solve the right problems involves asking the most basic questions facing all institutions:

- What business(es) are we in?
- What business(es) should we be in?
- What is our mission?
- What should our mission be?
- Who are our prime customers?
- Who should our customers be?
- How should we react to a major crisis, especially if we are, or are perceived to be, at fault?
- How will the outside world perceive our actions?
- Will others perceive the situation as we do?
- Are our products and services ethical?

The preceding questions apply universally; they pertain to all institutions, public or private. For this reason, throughout the book, I have chosen a wide variety of examples, which cut across the human condition, to illustrate how all institutions and sectors of society persistently engage in solving the wrong problems precisely.

The Four Steps of the Problem-Solving Process

Asking basic questions and challenging crucial assumptions are part of the problem-solving process. In addition, the problem-solving process has four distinct steps:

1. Acknowledging or recognizing the existence of a problem.

2. Formulating the problem.

3. Deriving the solution to the problem.

4. Implementing the solution.

All four steps are equally important in the problem-solving process. Because problem formulation has generally been neglected, which accounts for our relative ignorance of it, this book focuses almost exclusively on that step of the process. In contrast, the current educational system places extreme emphasis on the third step, deriving the correct solution to a given or preformulated problem—what I call an exercise. Depending on how they are defined, however, each step can be construed as an aspect of the other steps. For example, each step could be seen as a subpart of how the problem is initially formulated; if the initial formulation of the problem does not include implementation of the solution, you could say that the problem has not been adequately defined from the beginning.

Consider the following: The International Institute of Applied Systems Analysis (IIASA), located outside of Vienna, Austria, has produced literally thousands of computer models on every conceivable world problem, from energy consumption to the management of pollution. But very few of these models have ever been used! The sad thing is that they were all intended to help solve the world's enormous problems. The formulations of the initial problems, however, mainly considered *only* physical variables and processes; they did not consider political factors, such as political resistance to implementing the theoretical solutions. For this reason, it is not clear what the models have accomplished besides providing employment for the model builders.

Although all four steps of the process are crucial, let's focus for the moment on the interactions between the second and the third steps. In addition, let's suppose that we implement whatever solution we derive, whether it is correct or not. Figure 1-1 shows the four combinations of problem formulation and solution derivation.

		Step 3 of the Problem-Solving Process: Deriving the Solution	
		Right	Wrong
Step 2 of the Problem-Solving Process: Formulating the Problem	Right	1 Wise and Competent	2 Wise and Incompetent
	Wrong	4 Unwise and Competent	3 Unwise and Incompetent

Figure 1-1   Four Interactions between Steps 2 and 3 of the Problem-Solving Process

In Cell 1, we formulate the problem correctly and also derive the correct solution to it. In the business world, this is the fortunate situation where we formulate a correct business strategy and derive the correct implications—that is, actions to take—from it.

In Cell 2, we formulate the problem correctly, but we derive the wrong solution to it. In the business world, this is the unfortunately far-too-frequent situation where we may formulate a correct business strategy but we fail to derive the correct implications. That is, we are working on the right problem, but we fail to draw the right conclusions.

In Cell 3, we formulate both the problem and the solution wrongly. When this occurs in the business world, we not onlyl formulate a wrong business,strategy but we also draw the wrong conclusions. In this case, the two errors may cancel each other out, leaving us with nothing but wasted time and energy, or they may reinforce one another, creating an even larger problem.

In Cell 4, on the other hand, we formulate the problem wrongly, but we derive the right solution to the formulation of the wrong problem.

Thus, in a business setting, we end up with a wrong business strategy, but we have derived the correct implications from it. Cell 4 covers the situation of solving the wrong problem precisely. It is the main concern of this book.

Critical Questions for You and Your Organization

Because this book is intended to be interactive, each chapter contains critical questions for you, the reader, and your organization. The questions are an integral part of the book; they are intended to help you master the ideas contained in the book and also to apply them to your organization.

1. Identify three or more cases where you and/or your organization solved the wrong problem precisely. In each case, why did this occur?

2. In retrospect, what would have been the right problem formulations and why were they not formulated?

3. How can downsizing be the wrong formulation of an organization's problems? Total Quality Management?

4. How do downsizing and TQM have to be formulated, or reformulated, to make them the right problems for your organization?

CHAPTER 2

The Error of the Third Kind: Solving the Wrong Problem Precisely

SELF-EVIDENT, *adj.* Evident to one's self and to nobody else.
  —Ambrose Bierce,
   The Devil's Dictionary

THE TYPICAL COURSE IN STATISTICS teaches students the concepts of Type I and Type II Errors and how to compute them. Most students, however, are never taught that there is a much more fundamental and important error that pertains to all problems: this is the Error of the Third Kind, also called the Type III Error or E_3 for short.[1] The Type III Error is a little known but vitally important concept; it is the error associated with solving the wrong problem precisely.[2] There are five categories of E_3 errors, which I describe in detail later in this chapter, but first let me give a brief explanation of Type I and Type II Errors and some examples of Type III Errors.

Suppose over the course of a semester we give standardized reading tests to students in two different classes. Suppose that the two classes are evenly matched at the beginning of the term, that is, their initial average reading scores are virtually identical. Suppose that we compute the average reading scores for the two classes at various points over the term. Finally, suppose that the same teacher teaches both classes but uses two different methods of teaching reading. Given these suppositions, the assumed question to be answered becomes whether one teaching method is superior to the other.

The beginning student in statistics is taught that there are two kinds of errors one can commit in testing hypotheses or solving problems like the one above. A Type I Error arises from saying that there are significant differences between the average reading scores of the two classes later in the term when there are not. A Type II Error arises from saying that there are no significant differences between the average scores later in the term when there are. In other words, there are always differences, however slight, between any two groups, methods of instruction, and so on, but the key question a researcher must answer is whether those differences are far enough apart to be meaningful.

To give another example, when pharmaceutical companies are testing whether a new drug is better than an old one, they are generally much harder on the new drug than on the old one. The performance of the new drug has to exceed significantly the performance of the old one before a pharmaceutical company will conclude that the new one is superior. Pharmaceutical companies are willing to make larger Type II Errors than Type I Errors. They are more willing to say that the new drug is not better than the old one, when in fact it may be. Pharmaceutical companies are thus prone to play it safe rather than pursue the risky strategy of backing a new drug or treatment, especially when an old known treatment "works." This is the case even when the old drug can be improved upon.

Since the concept of E_3 emerged only after Type I and Type II Errors had been formulated, it was designated Type III. If it had been formulated first, as it should have been, it would have more appropriately been called the Type 0 Error because it not only occurs prior to the Type I and II Errors but also is more basic.

Type I and II Errors come into play after the problem has been formulated. Type III Errors, on the other hand, relate to the process of formulating the problem. Type I and Type II Errors pertain to doing given things right. E_3 asks, What are the right things to do? E_3 is the error of "solving the 'wrong' problem precisely when one should have solved the 'right' problem."[3]

In the reading comparison, for example, critical variables could be seen as the time of day the class is taught (before or after lunch) or the season in which the class is taught instead of the teacher or the method of instruction. The problem could thus be defined quite differently, relating to motivation, time of day, or seasons instead of to a person (teacher) or a method (of reading instruction). A well-known joke captures the idea succinctly: "What good does it do to find the best arrangement of the deck chairs on the Titanic as it is about to go down?" Talk about the solution to the wrong problem!

Type I and II Errors come into play after the problem has been formulated. Type III Errors, on the other hand, relate to the process of formulating the problem.

Examples of Type III Errors

E_3 issues an important challenge to all problem solvers: Why get an exact solution to the wrong problem when an approximate solution to the right problem may not only suffice but be better? Indeed, far better an *approximate* solution to the right problem than an *exact* solution to the wrong problem! There are countless examples of E_3 errors in the business world. For the moment, let's consider three.

Option Trikaya Grey is a Bombay-based advertising agency that hit upon the clever idea of using Adolf Hitler as a big name to promote a new fast food product, Dosa King Snack 'n Rolls, a south Indian delicacy.

"Yo! Dosa King," a snarling cartoon *Fuhrer* exclaims in colorful ads prepared for Indian magazines and slick newspaper supplements, in which he shares space with Abraham Lincoln, Count Dracula and other famous figures gripping rolled dosas.

Basically, this product is being positioned as a "fun prod-uct," said account supervisor Nitin Tandon of Option Trikaya Grey. "These are people who wouldn't normally imagine having a dosa. They add fun to the product."[4]

In this situation, the problem was formulated as a marketing, pro-motional, or attention-grabbing challenge. The advertising agency clearly failed to consider other possible formulations or to challenge its own idea. To defend the use of Hitler's name as a "clever promotional idea," the agency had to make the dubious and implicit assumption that the "celebrity" of Hitler could be decoupled from his evil acts. By failing to challenge its own assumptions, Option Trikaya Grey became a party to the history of evil. The point: always ask whether your strategy is not merely efficient but ethical as well.

Consider another example: a house was listed for sale in the real estate section of *The Hollywood Reporter*, a trade paper devoted to the entertain-ment industry.[5] The seller's last name was Schindler. The real estate agent handling the sale thought it would be "cute"—this is a direct quote—to advertise it as "Schindler's Listing" in order to draw attention to it.

The ad certainly drew attention all right. The real estate firm received complaints protesting its tastelessness from the head of nearly every major Hollywood studio.

As is so often the case, an initial dubious action—to put it mildly— gave rise to a chain of dubious arguments and then further dubious actions. In defending the ad, and in attempting to deflect attention away from its tastelessness, the realtor asked, "Would there have been any flap at all if the seller's last name had been, say, Piano, as in [the motion picture] *The Piano*?" Of course there wouldn't—that's the whole point! Merely raising the question is proof of the muddled thinking of the realtor.

In this situation, the first part of the problem was formulated cor-rectly as attracting as much attention as possible to a property in the highly competitive real estate market of Southern California. The second part, however, was formulated incorrectly as the search for and use of almost any means to accomplish the end result. It was the failure to appreciate the inappropriateness of the means that makes the case of Schindler's Listing a classic example of solving the wrong problem precisely. In the process of attracting maximum attention in the shortest time possible, the realtor succeeded in offending and angering the largest potential pool of buyers.

The case of Schindler's Listing is also important because it reveals one of the major patterns associated with many dubious arguments. First, a half-baked, half-thought-out idea is concocted. In the case of the real estate agency, this is the notion that it would be "cute" to list the property as Schindler's Listing. Second, little or no thought is given to the fact that others may not see the idea in the same way. The initial idea then prompts a foolish action, in this case, the actual appearance of the ad. Next, the proponents are shocked to find that they have caused a moral uproar in the community. An argument is then advanced to justify the initial action, prompting a further deepening of the mess. Last, the proponents then act as though they were the real victims of the entire affair. Rarely does it occur to them that the only way to break the cycle is to admit frankly that their initial ideas or actions were outright dumb. Unless this is done, dumbness grows exponentially, and as a result, the problems are compounded. Each solution only makes the problems grow and become worse.

Popeye's Chicken provides yet another example that reveals the comic-tragic nature of many dubious arguments and the wrong-headed problem formulations and actions to which they lead. The chain was forced to pull its billboard ads, which read: "The Best Breasts in Southern California Without Plastic Surgery." The ad wasn't perceived as funny by women who had undergone surgery for breast cancer. Joe Scafido, vice president of marketing for Popeye's, was surprised that the ad drew such strong reaction: "We thought we were just poking fun. . . . We were just looking for a humorous spin. A lot of people in Southern California have plastic surgery."[6]

The Importance of Critical Thinking

Although they appear to be academic, the Type I, Type II, and Type III Errors are anything but. They pertain to the fundamental differences between critical and uncritical thinkers. Uncritical thinkers focus on and attempt to minimize Type I and Type II Errors; critical thinkers focus on the Type III Error before they get caught up in Type I and II Errors. In other words, critical thinkers first attempt to insure that they are working on the right problem before they attempt to solve it in detail.

How we initially formulate or define a problem, the actions we take, and the arguments we use to justify those actions are all inextricably intertwined. As a result, raising basic questions or doubts regarding problems, key actions, and arguments is always an important activity.

Because the above examples are so outlandish, we are tempted to dismiss them quickly. That temptation needs to be resisted. Why individuals and organizations constantly fall prey to organized stupidity and evil is the phenomenon calling for analysis. To a greater or lesser degree, all organizations commit such acts daily. The outrageous is thus important to analyze precisely because it allows us to see what is generally hidden in the so-called normal.

Consider a final example, which illustrates just how commonplace the outrageous is. On a recent European holiday, my wife and I visited the infamous concentration camp Dachau, which is located in the city of the same name. It is easily reached by a thirty-minute train ride from the city of Munich, Germany.

Upon embarking from the train, we found ourselves in a town square where buses were available to take us to the concentration camp. The square contained a highly visible sign with the name of Dachau printed on it, a small map of the town immediately below it, and several ads for businesses. On each side of the word *Dachau* was a McDonald's golden arch. Upon seeing this, my wife and I were totally taken aback.

Always ask whether your strategy is not merely efficient but ethical as well.

Did anyone think of the consequences of associating this highly recognizable corporate logo with one of the most enduring symbols of evil? Notice that the decision, whether conscious or not, to put the golden arches on the sign in the first place is an E_3 error. The problem: How do we make our logo highly visible? And the solution: Put the logo in prominent places. Talk about the solution to the wrong problem! Precisely because such decisions are often made without conscious consideration of their impact on others is why they are so important to analyze.

Type I and II Errors involve where the arches should be placed on the sign for maximum visibility, how big the arches should be, and so on. The Type III Error involves whether the arches should be placed on the sign at all. Thus, the Type III Error involves looking critically and consciously at the impact of decisions on others, and it is the absence of this critical thinking that makes its exercise so important. For instance, was the decision made at corporate headquarters to make the golden arches as visible as possible in every town in Europe? Did no one give conscious consideration to the fact that there were certain cities in which it would be better not to advertise or to have a visible presence? Probably no one knows for sure, but perhaps all of us can learn from the situation.

Five Categories of Solving the Wrong Problem Precisely

Five categories of Type III Errors occur repeatedly in all contexts (see figure 2-1). Each category is distinct in the sense that it identifies a particular instance of flawed or muddled thinking. Nonetheless, the categories are not independent; there are strong overlaps between them. In fact, each reveals a different aspect or dimension of a complex problem. For this reason, any of the examples used in this book could be used to illustrate any of the five categories.

Figure 2-2 is a list of broad strategies, which, depending on the particular problem, can be used singly or in combination to counteract each of the five types of E_3 listed in figure 2-1.

Type	Description
1. Picking the wrong stakeholders	Involving only a small set of stakeholders in the formulation of a problem; ignoring other stakeholders and especially their reactions.
2. Selecting too narrow a set of options	Selecting a limited set of problem-solving options; not considering a broader set of options.
3. Phrasing a problem incorrectly	Using a narrow set of disciplines, business functions, or variables in which to express the basic nature of a problem.
4. Setting the boundaries/scope of a problem too narrowly	Drawing the boundaries or scope of a problem too narrowly; not being inclusive enough.
5. Failing to think systemically	Focusing on a part of a problem instead of the whole system; focusing on the wrong part; ignoring the connection between parts and wholes.

Figure 2-1   Five Categories of Solving the Wrong Problem Precisely

Strategy	Description
#1	*Pick the right stakeholders* Never make an important decision or take an important action without challenging at least one assumption about a critical stakeholder; also, consider at least two stakeholders who can and will oppose the decisions or actions.
#2	*Expand your options* Never accept a single definition of an important problem; it is vital to produce at least two very different formulations of any problem deemed important.
#3	*Phrase the problem correctly* Never produce or examine formulations of important problems phrased solely in technical or human variables; always strive to produce at least one formulation phrased in technical variables and at least one phrased in human variables.
#4	*Expand the problem's boundaries* Never draw the boundaries of an important problem too narrowly; broaden the scope of every important problem up to and just beyond your comfort zone.
#5	*Be prepared to manage paradox* Never attempt to solve an important problem by fragmenting it into isolated and tiny parts; always locate and examine the broader system in which every important problem is situated; in many cases, the interactions between important problems are more important than the problems themselves.

*Figure 2-2   Five Strategies for Avoiding Solving the Wrong Problem
Precisely*

Category 1: Picking the Wrong Stakeholders

The Make-A-Wish Foundation is a premiere example of the first category of Type III Errors. One of the most powerful ways of critiquing the foundation's actions is to examine the arguments the foundation most likely used in justifying its initial actions.

It is important to understand that I am not contending that my reconstruction of the arguments represents those actually used by the foundation. I am saying that when an individual's or organization's actions are onerous, or perceived as such, then it is up to the offending party to defend itself against the kinds of arguments that I know from my experience will most likely be used against it. In other words, the arguments I have constructed are not entirely of my own concoction. They are based on my work in crisis management, which has taught me the kinds of attacks generated in response to an organization doing, or perceived to be doing, wrong.[7]

I believe the foundation's most likely implicit, taken-for-granted assumptions were that the teenager was the primary stakeholder, and further, because of the tragedy of a life cut short, the outside world would be extremely tolerant of his last wish. To fully justify the decision, it would also have to assume that (1) the wishes of a terminally ill child, no matter how dubious or onerous, warrant granting; (2) other stakeholders will not object because of their sympathy for a dying child, or their sympathy will outweigh their ethical and moral qualms; and (3) other stakeholders will essentially see the situation as the foundation does. The foundation most likely defined the problem as follows:

> How to grant the wish of a dying child as effectively as possible no matter how offensive it may be to others.

The all-too-common failure in such a situation is the inability to anticipate and gauge the reaction of other stakeholders. The error is not merely failure to "walk in their shoes," but far more seriously, failure to "get inside their heads." This is precisely why decision makers need to continually take the pulse of a broad range of stakeholders. This does not mean taking a perfect reading of other people's minds; it means using market research and the other best methods available to check out taken-for-granted assumptions about a broad range of stakeholders.[8]

A colleague and friend, Niraj Verma, identified what could have been the foundation's deepest assumption of all; and for precisely this reason, it is least likely to be stated explicitly. The Make-A-Wish Foundation's actions in effect assumed that the teenager was already dead. If he was dead, then he was beyond the pale of moral judgment. His wish should be granted even if it caused evil or harm to others.

In short, the assumption is this: we are allowed to relax ordinary moral standards whenever a life is tragically cut short. Just stating this assumption is almost enough to see how absurd it is. Granting the teenager's wish essentially dehumanizes him by removing him from ordinary moral standards, which are necessary if one is to be part of a human community. All humans, living or dead, are always part of some community!

Strategy Number One: Never make an important decision or take an important action without challenging at least one assumption about a critical stakeholder; also, consider at least two stakeholders who can and will oppose the decision or action.

How to accomplish and speed up the process of identifying key assumptions, as well as arguments, is one of the primary topics of this book, as is the more fundamental point of how to identify important problems whose stakeholder assumptions and arguments need to be challenged.[9]

Category 2: Selecting Too Narrow a Set of Options

I often use the following true story to illustrate this second category:

A manager of a tall office building is receiving a mounting number of complaints from the building's tenants as well as from their clients with regard to the long waiting times for elevator service. He decides to call in a consultant to advise him on what to do.

Whenever I tell this story, I stop here and ask the audience members what type of consultant they would choose if they were the manager of the building. The immediate, knee-jerk response for most people is an elevator or building consultant. And in fact, that is who the manager did call.

The consultant recommended three alternatives that most elevator or building consultants probably would: (1) put in new elevators, (2) stagger the old elevators between different floors, or (3) speed up the elevators. While these alternatives would decrease the waiting time, they would also make matters worse because the cost of executing any of them would almost equal the cost of tearing down the building and rebuilding it!

Typically, consultants' solutions create even worse subsequent problems. (Another example is a proposal made many years ago to solve the nightmare of traffic problems in Los Angeles. It would have been cheaper to rebuild the entire city of Los Angeles somewhere up the coast than to implement the proposed solution!)

Over the years that I have used this simple example, very few people have initially recommended a consultant other than a building or an elevator expert, undoubtedly due in part to the way the problem is posed. The presentation carries an obvious bias toward some kind of building consultant or engineer.

Once the manager's dilemma is stated as whether or not to implement one of the elevator consultant's alternatives, people start thinking of other options. Eventually, someone suggests a psychologist. But what does a psychologist have to do with buildings?

In the original statement of the problem, the manager is receiving a "*mounting* number of complaints from the building's *tenants* as well as from their *clients*." What is *mounting*? Does the number vary by the time of day or day of the week? Is the number the same for all kinds of tenants, people in general, or only some? Are some tenants more powerful than others, such that even though they are few in number, if they complain loudly, then the building manager has almost no choice but to attend to their concerns? Is it the absolute amount of time people have to wait or is it the perceived or relative amount of time?

Before tearing into or tearing down a building, it might be advisable to consider these questions from the standpoint of another type of consultant. And in fact, this is exactly what the manager eventually did:

> One tenant in the building is a psychologist who is puzzled by the complaints of visitors and guests as to the long waiting times. On comparing the waiting times to those of nearby buildings, the psychologist finds they are longer, but not significantly so. Upon studying the problem further, the psychologist recommends that the manager install large mirrors in the lobby so that visitors and tenants can occupy themselves while waiting for the elevators.

This is a perfect illustration of the second category of E_3. The elevator consultant assumed that the manager's problem was *in the building*. As a result, the consultant considered only a narrow range of options consistent with his initial assumption. The psychologist, on the other hand, con-

The elevator consultant assumed that the manager's problem was in the building. *As a result, the consultant considered only a narrow range of options. . . . The psychologist, on the other hand, considered the possibility that the problem was . . .* in the people.

sidered the possibility that the problem was not in the building but *in the people.*

The moral of the story is not that building, elevator, or technical consultants are always wrong and that psychologists or people consultants are always right. The lesson in this particular case is that the psychologist was "right" and the elevator or technical consultant was "wrong" because it is far cheaper to try the psychologist's solution than the technical solution. This does not mean the psychologist will continue to have the right solution for all time. At some point, the vanity effect of the mirrors may wear off, and as the elevators age, the waiting time may increase substantially so that the only option will be new elevators, if not a new building.

We can push the concept of consultants even further: under what conditions do you call an ethicist, a lawyer, a political scientist, a historian, or even a priest or rabbi? Ask yourself, what would make a problem ethical, legal, political, historical, or even spiritual? (We discuss these possibilities in a later chapter.)

Strategy Number Two: Never accept a single definition of an important problem; it is vital to produce at least two very different formulations of any problem deemed important.

There is a deeper reason for producing at least two very different formulations of a problem: to assess whether we are solving the wrong problem precisely, we must compare several formulations of a problem. A single formulation is a virtual prescription for solving the wrong problem precisely, especially because of the tendency to fall in love with our earliest formulation of a problem, consider it obvious, natural, and so on. Nothing human is so good or so perfect that it does not deserve to be challenged. There is no single formulation of a problem such that we can say with absolute certainty or finality, "This is it!" Because of the pressure of any one of innumerable factors, we may not always have the luxury or the time to challenge a particular formulation, but we are always well advised to do so.

There is an apocryphal story of an airman stationed in Alaska whose job was to monitor a radar scope that warned of potential Russian missile attacks coming over the horizon. One night the radar system sounded a shrill alarm indicating that a large object was indeed coming over the horizon. To push or not to push the Big Red Button that would start World War

III was the question! Not fully conscious of his reasoning, the airman decided not to push the button. He just couldn't believe that the attack was real. Fortunately, he was right. The big object coming over the horizon was the moon, which the radar system had "somehow" (there seems to be a "somehow" in everything that humans do) not been programmed to take into account!

Category 3: Phrasing a Problem Incorrectly

Intel, the manufacturer of Pentium chips, was forced, after first staunchly refusing, to recall all of its chips when they were discovered to contain a flaw that affected complex division problems.

The flaw was first discovered by an obscure mathematics professor at an equally obscure small college. He was performing esoteric calculations with prime numbers (numbers that are divisible only by 1 or themselves, for example, 1, 3, 5, 7, and so on). The area of mathematics in which he was working necessitated performing billions of computations on ten-digit numbers.

Intel claimed that the errors associated with its chips were extremely rare. They would show up only in every few billion calculations. But since the professor was performing billions of calculations, he was in a perfect position to discover the problem. (The error later turned out to be more common than Intel first admitted.)

The professor alerted Intel, and after receiving an unsatisfactory response, he went public. He used the Internet to alert others and to inquire whether they had experienced the flaw as well. The Internet was soon abuzz as others quickly discovered it.

Intel refused to recall its chips even though customers were complaining strongly. In effect, Intel put the burden on its customers to prove that their applications were critical enough to warrant a replacement. What a clever marketing and public relations (PR) ploy! What better way to alienate customers.

The situation quickly escalated to a crisis when IBM, which used Pentium chips in its personal computers, announced that it would no longer purchase them. Only after the howls of protests from consumers reached a crescendo did the company finally agree to replace all chips, no questions asked. Intel had created a PR nightmare for itself.

This case is a model for how *not* to manage a crisis.[10] First, it is never advisable to alienate customers. As obvious as this is, maybe it was not obvious to the engineering culture that drives Intel. To Intel's engineers, the customers were reacting emotionally, and hence, irrationally. Intel's engineers reasoned as follows, "If a customer's application wasn't critical enough to warrant a replacement, why then would he or she rationally want one?" By eschewing emotions, Intel's engineers were unable to understand the reactions of the customers.

Intel defined its problem in purely technical terms, as a computer applications problem. It did not define it in human terms: users had fears and anxieties that needed explicit acknowledgment and attention. Without this attention, one of the most vital links in the chain between the manufacturer and its customers—trust—was broken. As a result, Intel committed one of the classic forms of solving the wrong problem precisely: defining a problem as technical when it was human.

Saddest of all, this story shows that in this situation, Intel, one of the companies most responsible for thrusting us into the Systems Age, didn't really understand systems. Systems are not composed of complex technologies alone, linked together in even more complex ways. Systems are composed of the interactions between organizations, people, and technologies. While technologies may be rational—and even this is assuming a lot—organizations and people are certainly not completely rational.

In sum, Intel phrased its initial problem using too narrow a set of disciplines—in this case only one, technology. The inevitable consequence was that the problem quickly turned into a major crisis, which ended up costing the company half a billion dollars, much more than it would have if Intel had initially offered to replace all chips with no questions asked.

Strategy Number Three: Never produce or examine formulations of important problems phrased solely in technical or human variables; always strive to produce at least one formulation phrased in technical variables and at least one phrased in human variables.

The language or variables in which we cast the problem is one of the most important determinants of its solution. It is also one of the most important determinants or predictors of future problems.

Category 4: Settng the Boundaries/Scope of a Problem Too Narrowly

The fallacy of solving the wrong problem precisely is not confined to a single walk of life. It is frequently found in areas where one would least expect it.

Recently, scientists at the Scripps Institute of Oceanography in San Diego were shocked to find that their proposal for studying global warming produced political opposition and moral outrage.[11] The scientists wanted to place huge speakers under the ocean to boom signals at very high sound levels between California and New Zealand. The speakers would transmit sounds starting in 1995 and continue until 2004. Since temperature affects the speed at which sound travels in water, the scientists hoped that the experiment would detect global warming, if it is occurring. The scientists proposed such a large-system experiment because a phenomenon that affects the whole planet, such as global warming, requires a large portion of the earth to test for the effect.

But the scientists didn't think systemically enough. They drew the boundaries of their system—and thus the problem—too narrowly. If they had thought more broadly, then they would have included the larger political and moral systems in which every human action is situated. Because they didn't do this, they were shocked to find that environmentalists were strongly opposed to their plan. Environmentalists were concerned that the sounds would disrupt the navigational systems of whales and other sea creatures and, hence, do them irreparable harm. The irony, of course, is that environmentalists are also intensely concerned about global warming and should have been supporters of the experiment. And they would have been if the experiment had been designed properly.

The language or variables in which we cast the problem is one of the most important determinants of its solution.

The saddest aspect of the entire affair is that the experiment may not even affect whales. However, because the scientists did not think of the broader political ramifications early on, it may be too late to correct public opinion. The scientists involved are still not sensitive to public opinion because, like many of their colleagues (shades of Intel), they regard the public as "irrational." The public may indeed be irrational, but they still have to be dealt with.

This example shows clearly that the scientific or technical aspects of problems can no longer be considered in isolation. Especially in today's world, a problem's environmental and moral aspects must be considered as well. The oceanographers committed one of the other major categories of solving the wrong problem precisely. They defined the problem essentially or primarily as a scientific one when it also had large ethical, environmental, and political components.

An additional example: recently, severe criticisms prevented the Disney Corporation from erecting a historical theme park outside of

Washington, D.C. The objections were not only mounted on environmental grounds but also on moral and financial grounds. The proposed location was near the sites of some of the bloodiest battles of the Civil War. To many, the Disney project thus represented a desecration of some of the most sacred and hallowed grounds of American culture. It was also close to properties owned by some of the wealthiest landowners in America.

In responding to the criticisms, Michael Eisner, chairman of the Disney Corporation, remarked, "We didn't do our PR homework." Eisner and Disney still don't get the point. They believe that their initial decision to build a historical theme park is validated by the eagerness of other locales to get their business. They still persist in bounding the problem too narrowly. They define it mainly in economic terms when it has significant ethical and political components.

Strategy Number Four: Never draw the boundaries of an important problem too narrowly; broaden the scope of every important problem up to and just beyond your comfort zone.

Category 5: Failing to Think Systemically

One of the most important examples of this category of E_3 is the Exxon Valdez oil spill in which Exxon attempted to place full blame for the catastrophe on the skipper, the infamous Captain Joseph Hazelwood. Exxon wanted to believe that only one part of its complex system was completely responsible for the entire system's failure or success.

In mid-September 1989, I attended a major conference on crisis management in New York City. The opening session, which occupied the entire morning, featured three main speakers: the lieutenant governor of the state of Alaska, the president of Exxon Shipping, and the officer of the U.S. Coast Guard responsible for the waters around Alaska. The purpose of the conference was to ascertain what lessons, if any, had been learned from the spilling of over ten million gallons of oil in the Bay of Valdez so that such disasters could be avoided in the future.

Not surprisingly, the lieutenant governor and the Coast Guard officer were much more candid and open in admitting errors and the lessons that needed to be learned than the representative from Exxon. Even at the conference, there was not much progress.

The president of Exxon Shipping, William Stevens, was responsible not only for overseeing the tanker Exxon Valdez, but also for managing the cleanup. Given his position, I was not surprised by his response to a question I asked him:

> Mr. Stevens, in every major disaster that has been studied to date, the entire management structure and culture of a company have been found to be major contributing causes. Rarely is the end link in the chain, in this case Captain Hazelwood, *solely* responsible. What then is Exxon doing to examine the parts that were played by its management and culture so that the same disaster will not happen again?[12]

Stevens denied vehemently that Exxon's management structure or culture was at fault in any way. It was purely a case of individual, human operator error. After all, if Exxon were at fault, then potentially the whole system would have to be overhauled. As a result, it was much easier to place full blame on a single defective part.

At the closing session of the conference, Stevens was called a fool by one of the members of the audience, who, significantly, was not an academic but a corporate executive. (Corporate executives made up approximately half of the attendees at the conference.) Stevens was called a fool because it was executive management, not Hazelwood, which, some weeks prior to the disaster, made the critical decision *not* to reexamine its preparations for a major spill. The likelihood of a spill was judged too small to warrant further precautions. The fact that one hadn't occurred justified lowering the probability of future spills. A perverse variation of Russian roulette was operating: the more times one had survived a gun fired at one's head, the safer it was to fire it another time!

What really raised the hackles of many in the audience was an earlier, angry remark made by Stevens: "What would you have had Exxon do, protect every single inch of the Alaskan coastline? That's patently impossible!" The answer to this question, of course, is no. (Notice the implicit E_3: either one protects every single inch or does nothing at all. The two extremes are not only false options but also quite misleading.)

Stevens's question obfuscates an essential point: it may be patently impossible to protect every inch of a fragile coastline, but one is certainly obligated to protect the most vulnerable part (two million gallons of oil flows into and out of the Port of Valdez every day), and Exxon had promised to protect Valdez as a condition for being granted the license to operate in the region in the first place. Exxon had promised that the necessary equipment would be there to prevent a spill as well as to clean up in case a spill occurred. Thus, the true options are differing proposals for how best to accomplish Exxon's obligations.

Exxon knowingly reneged on its promise. It cut back on safety and maintenance when oil prices took a sharp downturn in world markets. Safety and maintenance were judged to be the most expendable parts of the entire operation, the best places to cut costs. As a result, the proper equipment was not there and what was present was improperly maintained and hence not up to the task. (Safety is generally one of the first casualties of downsizing. This is precisely why the unreflective use of downsizing is so dangerous and how it can lead to Type III Errors.)

For another example, politicians regularly use this category of E_3. They define problems such that all blame or fault is placed on only one part of a complex system. Politics may indeed provide the quintessential examples of solving the wrong problem precisely. Consider, for instance, this story from the 1996 presidential campaign:

> Addressing a rally outside the Omaha Police Headquarters, Mr. [Robert] Dole declared: "Unlike the liberals, I don't think society is to blame for crime—I think criminals are to blame for crime. In my view, killing is caused by killers, robbing by robbers, drug-dealing by drug-dealers. That's what it's all about."
>
> Mr. Dole painted himself as much tougher on crime and criminals than Mr. Clinton. He offered no new solutions to the problems he described, instead running down Mr. Clinton to such a degree that he even blamed him for the weather. "The seasons are all mixed up," Mr. Dole asserted in the snappy morning chill. "That's what Clinton has done for us."[13]

Strategy Number Five: Never attempt to solve an important problem by fragmenting it into isolated and tiny parts; always locate and examine the broader system in which every important problem is situated; in many cases, the interactions between important problems are more important than the problems themselves.

Conclusion

The ideas in this chapter can be summarized as follows: (1) *what is not worth doing is not worth doing well,* and (2) *what is worth doing is worth doing well.*

The concept of E_3 forces us to jump up a level in abstract thinking. It asks us to look at the big picture—the whole forest—before we get caught up in the individual trees. It asks us to consider explicitly various ways of looking at an issue or problem before we settle on a particular formulation. As a result, we want to delve more deeply in the succeeding chapters into each of the errors we have identified.

Critical Questions for You and Your Organization

1. Give an example of each of the five categories of E_3 that you or your organization has committed.

2. In each case, why did E_3 occur?

3. Do you and your organization regularly commit one type of E_3 more often and more regularly than the others? Why?

4. How could the use of each of the five ways of avoiding E_3 have been helpful to you and your organization?

5. Construct other arguments that would have led the Make-A-Wish Foundation to the same actions it took; to different actions.

How to Solve the Right Problems

PART TWO

Part two goes into depth about the five categories of solving the wrong problem precisely, how to avoid them, and thus how to formulate a problem correctly.

Chapter 3 discusses how to pick the right stakeholders, chapter 4 how to expand your options, and chapter 5 how to phrase a problem properly.

Chapters 6 and 7 discuss how to think systemically—expanding the boundaries of a problem and managing the paradoxes that are inherent in any problem in today's world.

Picking the Right Stakeholders

"I'm here to remind you that taste is a highly individual issue," [General Manager Bob] Moore [of Los Angeles radio station KLSX] says in [an] editorial. "What is objectionable to some people is not to others. If you don't like what you hear, turn to another station or turn the radio off. Unfortunately, one special-interest group is trying to limit our free choice . . ."

Moore's action is the latest volley in a controversy surrounding [radio talk show host Howard] Stern, who on April 3rd [1995], in the wake of the fatal shooting of Latino singing star Selena, made derogatory comments about her tejano music and the people who like it, joking that her fans "live in refrigerator boxes . . . like to make love to a goat and . . . like to dance with velvet paintings and eat beans."

Stern said his comments were in jest, but Latino organizations in Texas and California expressed outrage and have sought to get stations and advertisers to drop him.

> —Claudia Puig,
> *Los Angeles Times*

House Majority Leader Dick Armey (R-Tex.) touched off a political firestorm . . . by referring to Rep. Barney Frank (D-Mass.) as "Barney Fag" during a radio interview.

The Texas Republican later angrily denied using the slur, which was recorded by several radio networks, and blamed the news media for reporting the incident.

Armey said that his utterance was neither an intentional insult nor a slip of the tongue, but an accidental sound that came out as he mispronounced the name of the Massachusetts Democrat, who is gay. He quickly apologized to Frank, but the liberal Democrat later told reporters that he could not accept it.

"I'm representative of a lot of gay people and lesbians who are a lot more vulnerable than I am to prejudice and so I have an obligation not just to shrug my shoulders and laugh it off," Frank said. While accepting Armey's assurances that the remark was not intentional, Frank said that he could not believe that it was a result of any difficulty that Armey had in pronouncing his name.

"There are a lot of possible ways to mispronounce my name but that one, I think, is the least common," adding that it strained credulity to imagine that "this was the result of his tongue hitting the wrong teeth with the wrong action of the chin."

> —Michael Ross,
> *Los Angeles Times*

In the latest exercise in questionable judgment to hit the O. J. Simpson case, defense attorney Robert L. Shapiro handed out fortune cookies to two writers at the courthouse, allegedly telling them "These are from Hang Fung restaurant."

At the time Shapiro handed out the cookies, . . . senior police criminalist Dennis Fung, who is Asian-American, was in the midst of a bruising cross-examination by Shapiro's colleague Barry Scheck.

> —*Los Angeles Times*

THE FIRST CATEGORY of E$_3$, picking the wrong stakeholders, pertains to involving only a single stakeholder or small group of stakeholders, or ignoring stakeholders altogether, in the formulation of a problem. A stakeholder is any individual, organization, institution, or even whole society that can affect or be affected by the actions of any other stakeholder. A stakeholder is one who has a stake in the actions of other stakeholders.

One of the most important points about stakeholders is that as all institutions and societies have become more complex, the number of stakeholders that can affect or be affected by decisions has increased enormously. (To use a term from chapter 2, the number of stakeholders that must now be considered has become increasingly "unbounded.") For this reason, the term *stake*holder is much broader and more encompassing than the term *stock*holder. *Stock*holders are merely one important class of *stake*holders.

Stakeholder Analysis

Columns one and two of Figure 3-1 give examples of different types of stakeholders. Most stakeholders are a combination of one or more elements of each of the columns simultaneously. For instance, one can be both an enemy and a legal expert at the same time; or one can be active, powerful, and a competitor at the same time.

Figure 3-2 is a tree diagram that illustrates how stakeholders are typically ignored or misrepresented. It can also be thought of as a labyrinth or a cave. At the entrance to the cave is an issue, problem, or situation we face. As we proceed further and further into the cave, we come to a series of branches illustrated by the levels in the figure. At each branch or level, we have to make a choice to go one way or another. If we go one way, we reach a particular outcome. If we go another way, we reach a different outcome. The various paths (as represented by the arrows in the figure) can be thought of as the reasons or the processes by which we make a particular decision to go one way or another. The different levels can be thought of not only as distinct outcomes but also as different considerations or questions we have to respond to in order to keep moving. Hopefully, as the result of enough correct choices, we eventually reach the final outcome, or the correct solution to our problem.

Box 1 in Figure 3-2 indicates that our implicit, taken-for-granted assumptions, conscious and unconscious, direct us to narrow the broad set of stakeholders shown in Figure 3-1 to those we typically feel comfortable considering. This smaller set, which is indicated by box 2, represents the particular stakeholder pool we typically consider in analyzing various problem situations. The vertical path from box 1 to box 2 indicates that implicit assumptions and arguments narrow the broad set of stakeholders in figure 3-1 to the ones we will actually consider in a particular situation. The two arrows from box 2 to boxes 3 and 4 indicate that the next sorting of stakeholders occurs when we divide them into those whom we consider relevant versus those we consider irrelevant. In different terms, we sort

By Stance	By Functional Role
Active	Competitor
Ally	Controller
Collaborator	Customer/Designer
Enemy	Information Handler
Friend	Legal Expert
Hero	Middle Manager
Opposition	Plant/Technology Operator
Passive	Political Activist
Powerful	Regulatory Agency
Rescuer	Researcher
Supporter	Stockholder
Weak	Supplier
	Support Provider (Fire/Health/Police)
	Top Manager
	Worker

Note: Most stakeholders are a combination of one or more elements of each of the columns simultaneously.

Figure 3-1 Different Types of Stakeholders

stakeholders into two classes: those who are high in power versus those who are low in power.

Once we have sorted stakeholders as to their relevance or power, we sort them into groups we consider similar to us versus those we consider dissimilar. This is represented by boxes 5, 6, 7, and 8.

Figure 3-2 shows the consequences of sorting stakeholders into the various categories. We assume that relevant and similar stakeholders will provide strong support for our actions and policies; relevant but dissimilar stakeholders will provide strong opposition; irrelevant and similar

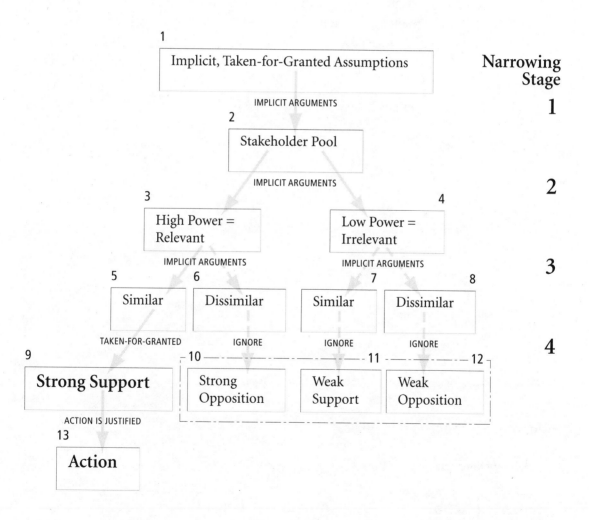

Figure 3-2   Narrowing Stakeholders through Implicit Stakeholder Analysis

stakeholders will provide weak support; and irrelevant and dissimilar stakeholders will provide weak opposition.

The important thing about Figure 3-2 is that it represents our implicit, if not often unconscious, analysis of stakeholders. In many cases, boxes 10, 11, and 12 are not considered explicitly at all. This is indicated by the dotted line around boxes 10, 11, and 12. We mainly consider those stakeholders who are important to us and think like us. They are taken as providing strong support, or justification, for our final actions, as indicated by box 13.

Figure 3-3 shows that an E_3 can occur on at least four levels. An E_3 is the result of the implicit arguments that we give at each stage for narrowing the initial pool of stakeholders, as well as the arguments about whether we consider stakeholders to be relevant or irrelevant, similar or dissimilar.

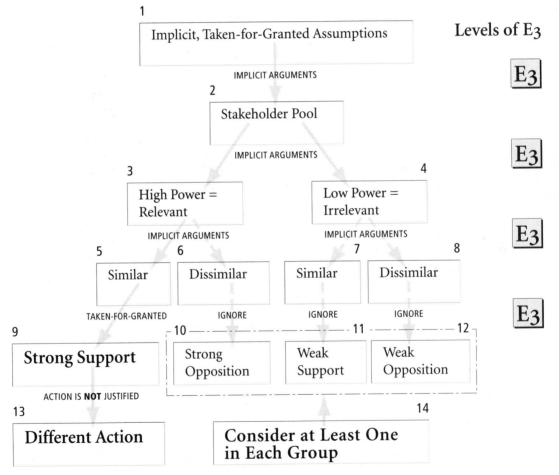

Figure 3-3   Determining Where E3 Can Occur through Explicit Stakeholder Analysis

Figure 3-3 also shows that to avoid an E_3, we should consider at least one additional stakeholder in boxes 9, 10, 11, and 12. One of the best ways to see this is to consider negative as well as positive examples of the treatment of stakeholders. How we treat stakeholders reflects our assumptions about their relevance, power, and similarity to us—assumptions that may not be true. Each of the following examples reveals the importance of challenging the implicit assumptions and arguments that we make at each stage of Figures 3-2 and 3-3 and how those assumptions and arguments lead to either the commission or omission of an E_3.

When We Assume That Stakeholders Are Just Like Us

One of the worst forms of E_3 occurs when we insult a group of stakeholders. In committing this type of E_3, we are implicitly assuming that a larger body of stakeholders is like us and shares our views (that is, the stakeholders are similar), while those who may be insulted are a smaller group and are not like us (that is, they are dissimilar).

The actions and statements of inflammatory radio personality Howard Stern and O. J. Simpson defense lawyer Robert Shapiro, which are cited in the epigraphs at the beginning of this chapter, are prime examples of this type of error. Stern played sounds of gunshots and made derogatory comments over a recording of the slain Hispanic singer Selena, whose life was tragically snuffed out by a deranged fan. Attorney Robert Shapiro uttered a stupid joke in reference to Los Angeles criminalist Dennis Fung, whose testimony in the O. J. Simpson trial was attacked strongly by members of the Simpson defense team. In addition, we can also include the case of U.S. Senator Alfonse D'Amato (R-N.Y.), who deliberately mimicked a Japanese accent in "poking fun" at presiding Judge Lance Ito in the first O. J. Simpson trial. Add to these two examples the stories in chapter 2 about the use of Hitler's name in promoting an Indian fast-food delicacy, the ad for Popeye's chicken breasts, and the real estate ad for Schindler's Listing, and we have an excellent sampling of this category of E_3.

The term stakeholder is much broader and more encompassing than the term stockholder. Stockholders are merely one important class of stakeholders.

Three Implicit Arguments

What do all of these examples have in common? They use the following, mainly implicit, arguments to justify an attention-grabbing idea or gimmick. The first part of the argument, which is most often unconscious, and hence rarely stated, is as follows:

If you want to grab and hold the attention of the public, you have to do something (call it x) that is bold or cute or so on; x is the best way to accomplish this.

The attention-grabbing argument leads to an implicit definition of the problem.

THE IMPLICIT DEFINITION OF THE PROBLEM

The essential problem is to grab or hold the attention of a fickle audience; the problem is thus to find the best way to accomplish this; compared to this, all other problems are insignificant or irrelevant.

In this case, an E_3 is the result of both the underlying argument (all of the public is similar to us so that there is essentially only one stake-holder) *and* the particular way in which the problem is defined (there is only one important problem). More precisely, the argument functions as a process, that is, it sets the path by which we go from box 2 to box 3 to box 5 to box 9 in Figure 3-2. It thereby limits the number of stakeholders we consider. If there is to be any hope of avoiding this kind of E_3, then it is absolutely vital that we bring to the surface the underlying arguments that produce it.

The attention-grabbing argument is merely the first part of a larger pattern. The second part, which is also rarely made conscious, and hence seldom made explicit, is as follows:

THE "OTHERS WILL SEE IT AS WE DO" ARGUMENT

What we see as attention-grabbing will not be offensive to others, that is, others will perceive it as we do.

THE NON-PROBLEM

The fact that others will see it as we do means we will not create a problem; therefore, there is no problem.

When others do not see it in the same way, then the third and final argument of the pattern kicks in:

THE "WHAT'S WRONG, CAN'T YOU TAKE A JOKE?" ARGUMENT

What's the uproar, what's the fuss all about? We only meant it as a joke, as satire.

The most effective way to get out of the situation is to explain that it was only meant as a joke; in other words, the new problem is merely one of "explaining it away."

All three arguments, and especially the problems that follow from them, represent major, unstated assumptions about stakeholders. These assumptions both shape and limit our perceptions of potential problems, as well as justify the actions we take (see Figures 3-2 and 3-3). If others perceive the world as we do, then not only are we justified in acting in certain ways (making derogatory remarks, uttering certain jokes), but also our actions will cause no problems.

Lesson Number One: Never assume that others will see a situation as you do.

Narcissism and E_3

All three of the preceding arguments are also perfect examples of the narcissism that is a fundamental ingredient in this form of E_3. Consider the following story.

A few years ago, a gunman wielding an automatic rifle attacked a school yard in the Stockton, California, area. A number of children were wounded; a few were even killed. In commenting on the situation in response to a television reporter's questions, specifically whether assault rifles should be banned, a gun owner replied, "If assault rifles were banned, I would be terribly inconvenienced." On hearing this argument—and I am giving it the extreme benefit of the doubt in calling it an argument—my outrage was immediate. Indeed, outrage is too mild to describe my reaction. How does one possibly weigh the "inconvenience" experienced by a parent who has just suffered the loss of a child against that of a gun owner who wishes to obtain an assault rifle as easily as possible?

The argument of the gun owner is a perfect example of narcissism. I am not using the term as it is ordinarily used, or better yet, misused. From a clinical standpoint, narcissism is not to be confused with self-love, as many who are diagnosed as narcissistic do not love themselves enough. Instead, they suffer from low self-esteem and, in this sense, do not have enough self-love or regard.[1]

In the sense in which narcissism applies to the gun owner, it is a character defect that manifests itself in extreme self-centeredness. The needs of the narcissist completely overwhelm the needs of others, even under the most horrible of circumstances, such as the killing of innocent children. This is why many arguments, and the E_3s to which they lead, are also unethical.

The recognition and formulation of a problem is not a purely intellectual matter. More often than not, we recognize problems and are motivated to solve them as the result of our strong moral outrage at a situation. The recognition and formulation of a critical problem is not ethically neutral. I am not asking readers to accept my particular moral outrage, but rather to express and to examine their own. (See the Critical Questions at the end of this chapter.)

The Growing Public Awareness of Insults

A piece in *Time* magazine in 1995 reveals that the arguments used to justify insulting various stakeholders have become so common and widespread that they can almost be reduced to a formula.

HOW TO APOLOGIZE JUST LIKE THE PROS

Uh-oh! You just insulted someone's ethnicity/religion/ sexual orientation and/or hinted the president might be in physical danger if he visits your state. Now what? A simple "Whoops!" won't cut it anymore, not when modern masters have elevated the post-gaffe backpedal to a sophisticated rhetorical art. Confused? Intimidated? Just follow these rules:

One of the worst forms of E_3 occurs when we insult a group of stakeholders.

1. Suggest the problem lies not in what you said but in how others reacted to it . . .

2. Allude freely to your own ethnicity. This tells the insulted, "I feel your pain . . ."

3. Explain that your cruel remarks were actually all in good fun . . .

4 Assure the people you have just insulted that actually, you think they are just swell . . .

5. Blame it on some mysterious physical or mental tic . . .

6. Finally, blame it on the media . . .[2]

Compounding the public's awareness of insults is the lack of secrets.[3] In today's world, it is truly foolish to believe that what one says behind closed doors or in private settings will remain there. The constant 24-hour-a-day, 365-day-a-year craving for news—everything everywhere is local news—has created a media monster whose appetite is voracious. What every public figure says is potentially page one news in the *Los Angeles Times, Wall Street Journal, New York Times,* or *Washington Post* or a lead story on CNN or the six o'clock "Action News." It is the height of arrogance, conceit, and foolishness to think otherwise. Thus, the E_3 is not only the tasteless joke or initial comment itself but also the presumption that it will stay private and not see the light of day. Again and again, the problem is in the initial assumption that what is said will not create a problem.

Lesson Number Two: Never assume that what is said behind closed doors will remain secret.

The public's awareness of insults is matched by its cynicism toward apologies. Why? Trust in public figures reaches new lows daily. We have been exposed and overexposed to the deceit and lies of those in high places for decades. Few public figures understand that they are part of a larger pattern. A single public official may not have been directly part of Nixon's lies during Watergate, but all of us are part of an enduring and larger pattern of deceit. In a word, the environment for lies, jokes, and deceit has been saturated. Like an ocean that can tolerate large amounts of pollution until it can no longer accept one more drop, our tolerance for deceit has reached its saturation point.

The current climate in America, with its cacophony of talk shows, each new one more "in your face" than the previous ones, has produced a general environment where everyone shouts but no one listens. Individuals go on television to reveal shamelessly their innermost secrets and embarrassments in order to grab their five minutes of fame. But most are participating in exhibitionism; few talk straight.

Our leaders have been groomed and overgroomed to talk and to think in slick sound bites. But true repentance is not the stuff of sound bites, which is precisely why apologies don't cut it anymore. Rare is the kind of candid admission by former Chrysler Chairman Lee Iacocca, who in responding to the fact that odometers had been falsely set back said, "It happened; it shouldn't have happened; it won't happen again!"

Given the public's awareness of insults and cynicism about apologies, the biggest dubious argument used to justify insulting stakeholders is this:

Our apology will be accepted at its face value because we're perceived in a different light from everyone else.

Expanding the Pool of Stakeholders

Let's now look at two situations in which managers dealt with problems involving stakeholders in a way that avoided committing an E_3.

Walter von Wartburg of CIBA

When I first met him, Walter von Wartburg was head of Issues Management for the Swiss chemical conglomerate CIBA. Because CIBA takes issues management seriously, Walter reported directly to CIBA's president and CEO. Essentially, he was a top level "mess strategist" for the entire organization.

I met Walter some ten years ago in New York City at a crisis management conference. Walter was giving a talk on issues management, illustrating it with several examples from CIBA. One in particular caught my fancy because it illustrates his novel approach to problem solving. It is particularly relevant here since it is an excellent example of reaching out to and including stakeholders whose publicly stated goals are different from those of an organization.

A few years before, CIBA had been picketed by the German Green Party. Two party members had ascended a six-hundred-foot smokestack and were in the process of unfurling a huge banner stating that CIBA was harmful to the environment. As Walter related the story, his eyes twinkled with amusement and excitement. He laughed as he said what the typical corporate response was to such incidents, "Red Bandit to Blue Bandit: locate the enemy and shoot them out of the skies!" Walter was not only well aware of the typical response, but he was equally aware how it usually backfired, for it played precisely into the hands of the "enemy." Worse, it created enemies where there were none before. He was thus determined to do something quite different.

Walter sent a corporate emissary up the smokestack to ask if the two Greens would come down because CIBA was worried about their safety. They could leave their banner up if they would just agree to talk. If they didn't want to come down, could CIBA at least help to insure that they were properly anchored to the smokestack so that they wouldn't hurt themselves? The two Greens eventually agreed to come down and talk over tea.

If the Greens had not responded to Walter's request to come down and engage in conversation, or if they had engaged in criminal actions, then the option of using force was always available. But why use force immediately without trying other options?

CIBA meets frequently with environmental and interest groups of all kinds. While it does not agree with or give in to every demand, it does take what is said seriously. If there are charges that CIBA is polluting in a certain area, then CIBA conducts tests to verify the charges. If the charges are true, as they sometimes are, then CIBA fixes the problem instead of denying or dodging it.

Notice how CIBA's actions stand in sharp contrast to those of other prominent organizations, such as General Motors (Corvair), A. H. Robins (Dalkon Shield), and Nestle (infant formula), which have all faced major crises.[4] In these cases, the offending organizations knew that they had serious problems of their own making (defective products), and yet they chose to deny their problems vigorously by blaming them on consumers and troublemakers. Thus, the major strategy was one of impugning stakeholders instead of fixing problems.

Also notice the assumptions that were buried in Walter's strategy in responding to the Greens who had ascended CIBA's smokestack. He assumed that he and the Greens were similar enough that they could at least talk with one another. Further, by wanting to talk, he was assuming that what they had to say was relevant. As a result, Walter did not end up creating worse problems by solving the wrong one initially. In short, Walter didn't take the Greens' bait. What good would it have done for Walter to figure out the best way of storming CIBA's smokestack if storming was the solution to the wrong problem?

If there is to be any hope of avoiding this kind of E_3, then it is absolutely vital that we bring to the surface the underlying arguments that produce it.

Mark Kroeker of the Los Angeles Police Department

Mark Kroeker was a deputy chief in the Los Angeles Police Department (LAPD). He served just two layers below the chief of the entire department. He was an LAPD police officer for over thirty years before he retired to become the head of Bosnia's police force.

On March 3, 1991, Rodney King was stopped for speeding and subsequently he was beaten horribly by LAPD officers, the video of which has been played over and over again such that it has become an icon of police misconduct. Because of his extraordinary skills in responding to community needs and the high confidence the department had in him, Mark was transferred just two weeks after the Rodney King beating to head the Valley Bureau of the LAPD, the jurisdiction in which the beating occurred.

Mark spent two years healing the wounds of the Rodney King incident. He attended countless community meetings, lunches, and dinners. He met continually with community groups. He never defended the officers' misconduct toward Rodney King or acted defensively. Instead, he listened and worked sincerely to insure that another such episode would not happen on his or anyone else's watch. When, two years later, he left for his new assignment as head of the South Bureau of the LAPD, a breakfast honoring him for his efforts was attended by six hundred citizens of the San Fernando Valley. Many thought that he should have been appointed the next chief of the LAPD.

Mark is a role model for including external stakeholders, who have typically been excluded or considered irrelevant, in the formulation of an organization's policies. As a strong proponent of community policing, Mark does not assume automatically that the interests of the members of a community are different from the interests of those who attempt to serve it, in this case, the police.

As a result, Mark continually worked to elicit the community's perceptions and definitions of the LAPD's problems. He worked not only to solve the problems he perceives but also to incorporate the perceptions of others into both the formulation of and the solution to important community problems.

> *Lesson Number Three:* Don't respond to stakeholders as if their actions or demands are totally unreasonable; don't respond to stakeholders in a way that leads them to act even more unreasonably; always ask what you can do to reduce, and not increase, the tension inherent in any situation.

> *Lesson Number Four:* Listen sincerely to your opponents by opening your mind and closing your mouth as much as is possible.

Lessons from Walter and Mark

Walter and Mark are premier examples of individuals who thrive in difficult situations. They each combine the general characteristics of a leader with a special adeptness at managing a problem to avoid committing an E_3. They each possess the following abilities, which allow them to include a wide variety of stakeholders in the problems they choose to solve:

- Thinking "outside the box." They are not afraid to think the unthinkable, ask "intelligent" dumb questions, challenge the conventional.

- Viewing the problems that everyone wants to avoid as opportunities. They thus instinctively know how to take advantage of crises.

- Being slightly off-key or at an angle to their organization's thinking. And yet they are able to remain credible.

- Practicing critical thinking in the best sense of the term. They avoid the latest management fads by sticking to the true fundamentals of management, and yet they are constantly changing and promoting change. They think in terms of "both/and," not "either/or" or "black and white."

- Brokering the definition of critical problems. They know how to elicit a broad range of views on important problems. They do not fall into the trap of acknowledging only one definition. They know that the definition of a problem is one of the most critical ingredients in its solution; therefore, before attempting to solve any important problem, they make sure that the organization buys into a robust, not a false or inadequate, definition of a problem.

- Nurturing "shadow constituencies" composed of leading thinkers both inside and outside their organizations. These constituencies continually provide them with a source of new and provocative ideas.

- Constantly bringing to the surface and challenging the key, taken-for-granted assumptions and beliefs of their organizations.

Conclusion

Those who are adept at including a wide variety of stakeholders in the formulation of important problems are constantly asking themselves the following uncomfortable questions:

- Whom do we typically include as well as exclude in our discussions and formulations of important problems?

- Who is absolutely unthinkable to include or exclude?

- How can we break through the unthinkable to broaden our definition of important problems?

Humankind continually vacillates between the following two unwarranted assumptions: (1) others are fundamentally like us and will react as we do to a situation, and (2) others are so completely different from us that there is no basis for mutual understanding whatsoever.

These two extremes of thinking exist in every field of human endeavor, from business to education to public policy. For this reason, it is important to identify and critique them relentlessly. Both are pernicious because they dehumanize us and those to whom we would relate. In both cases, the fundamental error is taking the narcissistic self as the primary, if not the only, stakeholder in all situations.

Critical Questions for You and Your Organization

1. In looking at Figures 3-2 and 3-3, which errors do you and your organization typically commit? Why?

2. Look at Figure 3-1 and make a list of stakeholders you and your organization regularly include in formulating problems. Why? Then make a list of those you regularly exclude. Why?

3. Make a list of stakeholders whom you and your organization have intentionally or unintentionally insulted or offended. Why?

4. What other arguments can you formulate that could justify the use of attention-grabbing strategies?

5. How could the lessons of this chapter be used by you and your organization in formulating problems more effectively?

6. What kinds of issues excite your moral outrage? How could what is morally outrageous to you lead to the wrong solution to an important problem?

7. The 1997 Super Bowl featured a provocative ad by Holiday Inn. The ad prominently featured a man who had undergone a sex change operation. He was attending his high school reunion. The ad was supposed to represent the changes that Holiday Inn was contemplating. If you were a top executive at Holiday Inn, would you have agreed or disagreed with running the ad? What arguments would you have used to justify running the ad? What arguments would you have used to justify not running the ad?

CHAPTER 4

Expanding Your Options

To every human problem there is a solution that is simple, neat, and *wrong.*
    —Walter Lippman

THE ELEVATOR PROBLEM WE DISCUSSED in chapter 2 is a simple but excellent example of the second category of E_3, selecting too narrow a set of options. In this chapter, we revisit the elevator problem and consider other problems as well.

Diagramming and Analyzing the Elevator Problem

To better understand this category of E_3, let's put the elevator problem in the form of a simple tree diagram. (See Figures 4-1 and 4-2.) Figure 4-1 shows that the formulation of the problem begins in box 1 with the detection of the number of complaints. This may sound trivial, but it is not. If we do not have a sensing mechanism, in this case the manager of the building, then we will not pick up the signals indicating that something is potentially wrong. In other words, we cannot "see" or "hear" data about a problem without the appropriate eyes or ears. In addition, we cannot receive, let alone make sense of, the data unless we have a mechanism that is especially matched to the particular kind of data we wish to receive. For example, a radio that can be tuned to only one frequency obviously cannot pick up others. Even more basic, a radio picks up only certain signals from the entire electromagnetic spectrum. It does not pick up every possible signal. Thus, the type of receiving mechanism we possess influences the kind of data we receive and process.

Once the data is received (box 1), we need appropriate tracking and comparative mechanisms to determine whether, over time, the number of complaints has been going up, staying

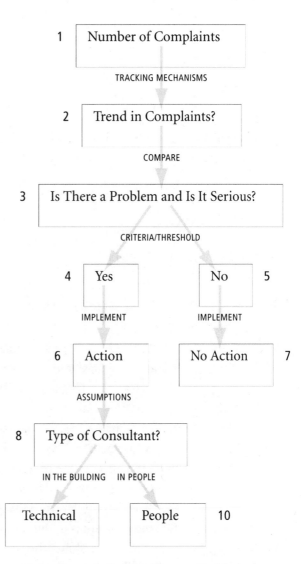

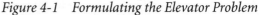

Figure 4-1   Formulating the Elevator Problem

the same, or going down. (The mechanisms are represented by the arrows from box 1 to box 2 and box 2 to box 3).

Next, if the number of complaints has been going up, we have to decide whether the number is serious enough to warrant action. That is, the number has to exceed some threshold as specified by some criterion. If the number does exceed this threshold, then and only then can a problem be said to exist. Notice once again all of the steps that go into the *formulation* of the problem, even before we attempt to solve it. In fact, everything in Figure 4-1 is part of the formulation of the problem.

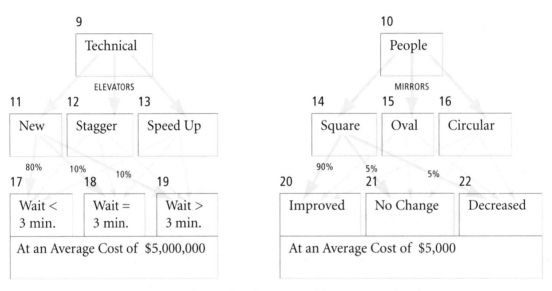

Figure 4-2   The Consequences of How the Elevator Problem Is Formulated

Once it has been determined whether a problem exists or not (boxes 4 and 5), we have to decide whether it is worth proceeding further or not (boxes 6 and 7). That is, a problem may exist, but for many reasons, we may wish to defer dealing with it. Once we have decided that the problem warrants action, however, we have to decide what type of advisor or consultant to call in. Again, the type of advisor presupposes a preliminary definition or formulation of the problem. In Figure 4-1, this is shown by the arrows from box 8 to box 9 and from box 8 to box 10. If we go to box 9, we are saying that the problem is in the building. If we go to box 10, we are saying that the problem is in the people.

Figure 4-2 shows the consequences of formulating the problem as a technical one versus a people one. If we formulate the problem as a technical one and hence call in a building or elevator consultant, we get the three recommended solutions shown in Figure 4-2: install new elevators, stagger the old ones, or speed up the old ones.

Figure 4-2 also shows that if we install new elevators, there is an 80 percent chance that we will have to wait less than three minutes for an elevator to arrive, a 10 percent chance of having to wait exactly three minutes, and a 10 percent chance of having to wait longer than three minutes.

If we stagger or speed up the old elevators, then we will get other percentages for waiting less than three minutes, and so on. These percentages are not shown in Figure 4-2 since they would unduly complicate the diagram.

Notice, however, that if we put in square mirrors (box 14), there is a 90 percent chance that we will improve the satisfaction of the building's occupants and customers, a 5 percent chance of no change or improvement in satisfaction, and a 5 percent chance that satisfaction will decrease.

Figure 4-2 also shows that the three outcomes do not fully represent the solution; cost is also a factor. Any one of the elevator consultant's recommendations has an average cost of $5 million. On the other hand, any of the psychologist's solutions has an average cost of $5 thousand. Quite a difference to put it mildly! In other words, the *price* of the solution is fundamentally part of the solution.

E_3 is choosing the wrong branch of the tree diagram in figures 4-1 and 4-2, which in this case means choosing the solution that costs significantly more.

Type III versus Type I and II Errors

E_3 is choosing the wrong branch of the tree diagram in Figures 4-1 and 4-2, which in this case means choosing the solution that costs significantly more. In other words, E_3 pertains to the choice *between* the two major branches. In more precise terms, E_3 is the error associated with saying that the technical formulation of the problem is the correct one when the psychologist's formulation is the more appropriate one.[1] This means that E_3 occurs at least as far back or up in the decision tree as the arrow from box 6 to box 8 in Figure 4-1.

On the other hand, Type I and II Errors for this problem pertain to the numbers far down on the tree, for example, the arrow from box 11 to box 17 in Figure 4-2. On the other branch of the tree, in the psychologist's formulation of the problem, the Type I Error consists of saying that the three differently shaped mirrors are not equally effective in lowering tenant dissatisfaction when they are equally effective. The Type II Error consists of saying that the mirrors are equally effective when they are not, that is, when one shape is actually more effective than the others. In the psychologist's formulation, the Type I and Type II Errors may not matter much since the shape of the mirrors may be inconsequential, both in effect and cost. In the technical formulation, however, the Type I and Type II Errors may matter since the three solutions may differ greatly in cost.

Once again, in the typical statistics course, a student learns how to compute Type I and II Errors, but these errors *only* come into play *once* a particular formulation of a problem has been chosen. What good does it do to find the best way of replacing or speeding up elevators if this is the solution to the wrong problem? The typical student almost never confronts this question because he or she is virtually never introduced to the concept of E_3.

The Importance of Problem Formulation

Figures 4-1 and 4-2 give the opportunity to reemphasize the importance of the formulation of a problem. In Figures 4-1 and 4-2, each of the separate branches of the tree is in effect a different formulation of the elevator problem. Problem formulation consists of the following:

1. The complete set of branches on a decision tree leading to the alternative outcomes that are seen as potential solutions.

2. The various outcomes themselves.

3. The processes, arguments, and assumptions we go through to get from one level of the tree to another.

4. The numbers on the very last branches of the tree, which represent the effectiveness of the various potential solutions.

5. The total benefits and costs associated with the potential solutions.

Understanding an Exercise versus an Ill-Structured Problem

The elevator problem also gives the opportunity to point out the difference between an exercise and an ill-structured or messy problem. If, for example, in Figures 4-1 and 4-2, we were given *complete* information on one and only one branch of the tree (technical or people) and asked to choose the option that is best, then we would have an exercise because it is bounded and structured. We would know the various options or potential solutions for one branch of the tree; we would know the relative efficiencies of the different options and the complete set of outcomes; and we would also know the values of the various outcomes relative to one another. In this case, the tree would reduce to a long pole we could slide down.

The elevator problem becomes an ill-structured or messy problem, however, if one or more of the branches of the decision tree are not specified. In this case, the processes, arguments, or assumptions that lead us from one branch to another would be highly tenuous or problematic. As a result, different stakeholders might well see different trees altogether. For instance, in presenting the initial discussion of the elevator problem, we could have formulated it from two entirely different and opposing technical perspectives. In the particular way it was presented, the psychologist's solution makes more sense. But if we had used two different economic or financial models to evaluate the cost of replacing the elevators, it might have turned out that the psychologist's solution was not the cheaper one in the proverbial long run.

The point is that an ill-structured problem, in contrast to an exercise, contains considerable unknowns. The branches of the tree of an ill-structured problem may be partially or completely unknown, and it may be possible to determine only some of the numbers (efficiencies, values) associated with the tree. Thus, an ill-structured problem may range from mildly unspecified, unknown, or indeterminate to severely unspecified.

The conclusion: you can ascertain whether you are committing an E_3 only by comparing two very different formulations of a problem. A single formulation of a problem is a virtual prescription for disaster.

Picking the Wrong Technical Formulation of a Problem

E_3 does not occur only when we pick a technical definition of a problem (for example, an engineer's) when a human definition (for example, a psychologist's) is more appropriate, or vice versa. E_3 occurs just as often when one technical formulation is more appropriate than another or when both are equally inappropriate.

All academic disciplines and professions heavily socialize their practitioners and students into particular ways of looking at the world. Sometimes the results are tragic; often they are humorous; at times, they are both.

Some years ago, I came across a study that showed how graduate training skews a person's basic perception of the world. A group of advanced medical students and an equal-sized group of advanced psychology students were each shown pictures of young infants and asked to describe their problems. The medical students saw medical problems, such as colic. The psychology students saw potential behavioral difficulties between the mothers and their infants.

Neither group saw the problems of the other group. As a result, no one posited that both types of problems might be operating simultaneously or that one led to the other. If a person can't see the problems associated with seeing the world from another perspective, then the person certainly can't see that these problems might be interactive, for instance, when one type of problem leads to another.

Although it might appear that the psychology students' definition of the problem was a human definition rather than a technical one, it is important to point out that it is technical. The psychology students' definition was stated in terms of the impersonal, academic, professional jargon of their discipline. Indeed, a discipline is always a tip-off that what follows will most likely be a technical description of a problem.

In contrast, human definitions are typically posed in terms of moral outrage or extreme emotion, as with the customers' reactions to Intel. Do not think that a problem definition is human merely because it comes from a social scientist. Because of their extreme desire to emulate the physical sciences, and thus attain "true" scientific stature, and also because of the generally low self-esteem of social scientists, they often try to appear harder than the so-called hard sciences.[2]

Four Perspectives on Any Problem

Figure 4-3 displays four perspectives on the formulation of any problem. All problems have significant aspects from each of these four perspectives. As a result, to ignore one or more of them almost guarantees that you will commit an E_3.

For instance, consider the following: The bombing of the federal office building in Oklahoma City on August 19, 1995, which took the lives of 168 people, was one of the most heinous acts in American history. It took a heavy toll on the American psyche because it literally and figuratively "shattered" some of the most fundamental assumptions about U.S. society.

First, because of their geographical location deep in the American heartland, the citizens of Oklahoma City assumed that they were protected, if not immune, from terrorism. Second, because of our deeply held assumptions about the nature of Americans, we took for granted that no U.S. citizen would commit an act of terrorism against his or her people.

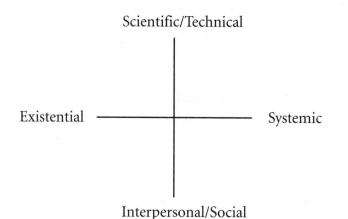

Figure 4-3   Four Perspectives on Any Problem

Third, it is literally unthinkable to most Americans that anyone would want to kill, or allow to be killed, innocent bystanders, especially children. An assessment of the Oklahoma City explosion—in particular what we can learn from it in order to prevent future tragedies—involves all four perspectives outlined in Figure 4-3.

The *Scientific/Technical* perspective concerns the scientific/technical causes of the explosion (for example, the nature of the explosives that were used and where the truck with the explosives was parked); the effects of the explosion on the building, given its design; and how other buildings could be protected, given what has been learned from the damage to the building. The Scientific/Technical perspective was also involved in the physical recovery of the victims, for instance, how to recover victims with as little harm as possible to the rescuers.

The *Interpersonal/Social* perspective concerns the psychological and social treatment of the victims, their families, and the larger community. This dimension involved the use of specially trained mental health workers who were skilled in grief counseling. It also involved mental health professionals who were trained to treat acute and extreme cases of stress and trauma. In many cases, it involved treatment of whole families, since a seriously wounded person affects the larger personal and social systems of which they are a part.

The *Existential* (or spiritual) perspective concerns some of the most basic issues of the human condition: meaning and purpose. Most of the time, these issues reside in the background; they are taken for granted. In cases of extreme tragedy, however, especially one that takes the lives of so many so quickly, including the lives of young children, basic issues surface with a vengeance: What is the meaning of what took place? How can we make sense of it? Why did it happen here to us at this time? What kinds of persons could do such a thing? How do we deal with the anger we feel toward those who did it? How do we honor the memory of those who died and yet get on with our lives? Because the existential questions—better yet, existential wounds—were so deep, they had to be not only acknowledged but treated properly. They could not be allowed to fester. If they had, they would have destroyed the "soul" of the city and the nation.[3] As a result, a national day of mourning was proclaimed. It was led by President Clinton and the Reverend Billy Graham. Through prayer and language that was explicitly spiritual, not necessarily religious, existential matters of the soul were addressed head on. This occasion was a fundamental part of the healing process. People had to be allowed not only to express their pain but to express it in such ways that it could be healed properly.

The last perspective, *Systemic,* concerns the fact that tragedies like Oklahoma City reverberate far beyond their geographic borders. They raise issues of national and even international security. They certainly raise fears nationwide and internationally. The fact that it is impossible to protect any facility or location completely is fodder for politicians, security experts, technologists, and others. That acts of terrorism are rarely isolated is another concern of the Systemic perspective. Most acts are part of a larger pattern; thus, detecting such patterns has become serious business. For instance, could and should the FBI have picked up the inevitable early warning signals of the Oklahoma City bombing, which in retrospect are seen to accompany every disaster? Would better national and international monitoring systems of radical and militia groups have helped, and so on?

What is it that is so frustrating about the bombing in Oklahoma City and all of the complex problems in today's world? They have significant aspects that involve every one of the four perspectives in Figure 4-3 simultaneously. If one of these perspectives is overlooked, or downplayed, then an essential part of the definition of the problem is missed. Thus, an essential part of the solution is missed as well. We have no choice but to approach all complex problems in terms of all four perspectives.

This does not mean that all four perspectives are equally important in all problems, although in principle they are present in all problems. The job of the problem formulator is to justify why one perspective or another is more important in a specific case.

Another important contemporary example of a problem is downsizing. For most organizations, downsizing is seen mainly as an economic necessity. In terms of Figure 4-3, the problem is thus primarily Technical in nature. Technical questions of corporate finance are primary, that is, how much will be saved if an organization's workforce is reduced by a certain amount?

But downsizing has aspects that tap into each of the other three perspectives. It has Interpersonal/Social aspects since it profoundly touches the emotions of the individuals and families who are affected. It has Systemic aspects because it affects the surrounding community in which every business is imbedded. And finally, it has deep Existential aspects because the victims of downsizing generally question their self-worth, since their sense of purpose and meaning, which is generally provided by their work, is shattered.[4] It is therefore not an exaggeration to say that downsizing generally forces a deep spiritual crisis on those whom it affects.

The Emerging Job of the CIO

To avoid an E_3, an organization must look at problems from more than one of the perspectives shown in Figure 4-3. This in turn requires an understanding of the body of knowledge associated with each perspective and a senior level person who can coordinate the use of this knowledge.

Scientific/Technical (or impersonal) knowledge concerns how and why things are the way they are. This knowledge is used to solve scientific/technical problems, and in addition, it is the foundation for pursuing a professional career in today's complex society.

Interpersonal knowledge refers to how we get along with and relate to other persons, our families, institutions, our society, and all of humankind. The basic issue connected with interpersonal knowledge is finding the balance between independence on the one hand and closeness and intimacy on the other. If we get "too close," we are swallowed up by others and lose our identity. If, on the other hand, we form no close relationships or cannot engage in intimacy at all, we are not fully human or developed.

Existential knowledge concerns the most basic questions everyone must answer for himself or herself: Why am I here? What is my purpose? What should I do to lead a satisfying life?

The conclusion: you can only ascertain whether you are committing an E_3 by comparing two very different formulations of a problem. A single formulation of a problem is a virtual prescription for disaster.

Systemic knowledge concerns our place in the broader context of the world, as well as the broadest context of human history and the entire universe. The questions are: Do our actions and ideas in the small context hold up in the large? Do they apply equally to everyone?

One of the most significant new positions that has been created in many organizations is that of the chief information officer or CIO. Unfortunately, given the importance of the job, it is a tragedy that its role and functions have not been better understood.

From the perspective of this book, the central task of the CIO is to manage E_3. In terms of the Scientific/Technical perspective, the CIO has to manage the various scientific and technical professions that will be used to define the problems an organization addresses. As we have emphasized, it is extremely dangerous to pick one and only one discipline or profession to illuminate a problem. Indeed, to the contrary, we have recommended strongly that for any problem, at least two very different ways of approaching it be constructed. Thus, one of the primary tasks of the CIO is to select at least two or more disciplines within his or her organization to bring to bear on important problems. This demands a CIO who is familiar not only with the physical sciences but also with the social sciences.

Figure 4-3 also leads us to the reformulation of other more established disciplines. For example, the head of the human relations department must manage the Interpersonal/Social and Existential perspectives and thereby becomes an integral part of the problem-formulating team of an organization. Thus the head of human relations is no longer limited to the traditional function of employee relations. In addition, the role of strategic planning must be broadened to include the Systemic perspective on problems faced by the organization.

Most fundamental of all, the CIO and the heads of human relations and strategic planning must be part of an executive problem-formulating team. It is not enough to consider each of the perspectives of Figure 4-3 in isolation from one another. They must be considered together in order to give complex problems the breadth they require.

Crisis Options

Unfortunately, most individuals and organizations, when they face a crisis situation, tend to narrow their options. This is especially tragic because every crisis calls for the exact opposite, the broadening and expansion of options. For instance, the strategies (or options) adopted by

GM (Corvair), A. H. Robins (Dalkon Shield), and Nestle (infant formula) in dealing with deaths due to the use of their products were primarily legal and public relations strategies. Only after it became abundantly clear to each of these organizations that it could not win in the courts of law or public opinion, that is, technically, did each finally turn to the only perspective that really counts with the public in major crises, the existential. In each case, the offending company finally had to "do the right thing." It had to act ethically, which meant withdrawing its products from the market, admitting its guilt and responsibility, and compensating the victims.

One of the unfortunate features of most crises is that the very option that is denied or resisted most vigorously in the beginning—the option for ethical action—is the one that is almost always adopted in the end. The longer an organization puts off adopting ethical actions, or when it is forced to adopt such actions after a protracted battle, the greater the chances that the initial crisis will grow. In addition, the chances are also greater that the organization will be perceived as a villain.

The Castle Problem: Expanding Options and Stakeholders

The following true story about a thirteenth-century castle presents a simple problem that shows how to apply the ideas of the last two chapters.

The castle, which had been surrounded and besieged for months by a powerful opposing army, was literally down to its last two sacks of grain. After these were exhausted, the inhabitants would either starve to death or have to surrender to the enemy and most likely be put to death. If you were the "CEO" of the castle, what would you do?

Most people who are given the Castle Problem recommend a series of options that have to do with rationing or stretching the consumption of the sacks of grain in the hope that buying more time will somehow lead to survival. While not entirely wrong, the generation of such options takes place within the particular formulation of the problem as primarily one of conserving known food supplies. It takes food at its face value, as a nutrient.

However, there is another view of food that leads to an entirely different set of options. This view reformulates food as a symbolic or strategic resource. Within this view, the castle's CEO reasoned as follows:

What does it matter if we have one or two sacks of grain?

What does it matter if we starve one or two days earlier if

One of the unfortunate features of most crises is that the very option that is denied or resisted most vigorously in the beginning—the option for ethical action—is the one that is almost always adopted in the end!

starvation is the most likely outcome that will occur sooner or later? Therefore, what if we do the unthinkable and throw one of the sacks over the wall? Would this not only signal our contempt for the enemy but also show them that after months of being besieged, we still have so much food that we can "afford" to waste some? Might not this action so demoralize the enemy that they will pack up and leave?

In this problem, a true series of options exists only when we produce at least two different formulations of the problem. I am not saying that the second formulation is necessarily better but that the two formulations are different enough that they give us a real choice. In examining various problem-solving options, it is never enough to expand them *within* a particular formulation of a problem. In addition, it is necessary to produce options from entirely different ways of viewing the problem. Thus, true options result only when we examine them *across* very different formulations.

Notice further how different formulations make very different implicit assumptions about stakeholders. In the first formulation, the assumption is that the castle's inhabitants, as well as the opposing army, see food as nothing more than a nutrient: "Food is food and nothing more." In this formulation, the inhabitants either starve to death or eventually surrender.

In the second formulation, the castle's CEO assumed that if he threw a sack of grain over the wall, the enemy would be demoralized by such an unanticipated action, but he didn't know this for sure. It was not, therefore, an easy formulation to sell to the castle's inhabitants. But he kept pressing with the challenge, "What have we got to lose? We'll either be dead sooner, or we'll be alive." This formulation does not assume that "Food is food and nothing more." In this formulation, food has a symbolic value as well.

There is little doubt that throwing a sack of grain over the wall is the riskier of the two formulations. However, on second thought, is it really? The point is that an assessment of risk, or any other variable, cannot be made independently of the formulation of a problem.

Conclusion

Following is a summary of the lessons of the Castle Problem, as well as the last two chapters:

1. Always seek to expand your problem-solving options *within* a particular formulation of a problem.

2. Always seek to expand your problem-solving options *across* or *between* different formulations of a problem.

3. The most important formulations occur when you consider the outrageous and the unthinkable; therefore, do not be afraid to challenge conventional notions.

4. Different formulations of a problem are based on fundamentally different implicit assumptions about key stakeholders. Therefore, state those assumptions as clearly and as boldly as possible.

5. As much as possible, challenge your assumptions about key stakeholders by reversing them. See if your solutions can stand up when key stakeholder assumptions are reversed.

Critical Questions for You and Your Organization

1. In terms of Figure 4-3, which types of problems do you and/or your organization typically concentrate on? Ignore? Why?

2. Consider an important problem that you or your organization has faced. Define the problem from all four perspectives of Figure 4-3. What does this tell you about the nature of problems?

3. What can you and your organization do to broaden the types of problems you need to consider?

CHAPTER 5

Phrasing Problems Correctly

For many years, most self-styled conservatives have contended that the depiction of sex and vio-lence on television and in movies promotes anti-social behavior. Now many people identified as liberals are saying that the preaching of hate and division, which is particularly evident on talk radio, contributes to a climate in which insane acts of violence such as the tragic bombing [in Oklahoma] on April 19th [1995] are more likely to occur.

Both groups are right about the potential effects of the messages that reach us through the electronic media. What is so curious is that each side seems willing to see the problem in only one portion of the media. . . .

One side [conservatives] would have us believe that violent speech and images are dan-gerous if they come out of a television set but not if they are emitted by a radio. The other side [liberals] tries to persuade us that such images can lead to trouble if they are issued from a radio but not if their source is a television. It is difficult to see how either side can have it both ways. Either words and images can affect behavior or they cannot.

—Robert S. McElvaine,
Los Angeles Times

IN CHAPTER 2, we said that the categories of E_3 are related strongly to one another; each is, in effect, a different perspective on a complex phenomenon. As a result, all of the examples that we use in this book could be used to illustrate any of the various categories of E_3. This chapter uses some new examples to show how the perspective we take on a problem influences the language we use and ultimately the responsibility we feel for that problem.

Language and Natural First Questions

The language we use is one of the most important determinants in the formulation of a problem. Our language, in turn, is heavily influenced by our education, scientific discipline, professional specialty, personal background, and so on, all of which affect the perspective we choose to take on a problem. (See Figure 4-3 on page 59.) As we will explain in more detail in chapter 8, each of the four perspectives in Figure 4-3 is used differently by different people. Each of the perspectives, besides being influenced by education and training, is an expression of a person's underlying personality.

The following story would merely be amusing if its consequences weren't so serious and if it were an isolated example. In an article entitled "How Many Species Inhabit the Earth?" zoologist Robert May poses the following question:

> If an extraterrestrial explorer were to land on the earth, *what is the first question it would ask? The alien would, I think, inquire about the number and variety of living organisms on this planet* [emphasis added]. Given that the earth's physical attributes derive from universal and essentially deterministic laws, the presumably well-traveled visitor would probably have seen countless similar worlds throughout the universe. But the warp of evolutionary forces and the weft of chance that cradle the rich tapestry of life on the earth are almost certainly unique.
>
> Surprisingly, we humans cannot even approximately answer the alien's query. Despite more than 250 years of systematic research, estimates of the total number of plant, animal, and other species vary widely, all the way from 3 million to 30 million or more. *Because no central archives exist, no one even knows how many species have already been named and recorded* [emphasis added].[1]

The preceding is amusing because we can readily think of innumerable other "first questions" that an extraterrestrial explorer might "naturally ask." The obvious or natural first questions depend on the asker's training. For instance, an alien with an ethical bent would naturally be concerned with how ethical the creatures are on this planet, how well they treat one another, and whether they have learned the secret of living well. An alien with a political bent might be interested in the nature, variety, and sophistication of the inhabitants' political systems, and on and on.

It is not that the zoologist is totally wrong. Rather, the narrowness of his approach is a direct reflection of his training. He fails to consider other natural first questions that other kinds of aliens might ask.

Once again, for the zoologist, the solution follows obviously from the initial statement of the problem:

> *Improving the catalogue of life will require a huge coordinated and sustained effort* [emphasis added]. I believe such dedication is warranted. Conservation will increasingly necessitate intervening in and managing ecosystems, along with making agonizing choices of where to concentrate such efforts. *Those actions will demand better information than is currently available* [emphasis added].
>
> Future generations will, I believe, find it incomprehensible that in the late twentieth century . . . our society has devoted *so little money and effort towards quantifying and conserving the forms of life that define the earth's unique glory* [emphasis added].[2]

If the problem is defined, as the zoologist defines it, as enumerating and preserving the diversity of species, then we invest money in its determination. But this would be to commit an E_3. Only by using several different perspectives can we be sure of having phrased the initial problem correctly.

The language we use is one of the most important determinants in the formulation of a problem.

The Language of Science versus the Language of Ethics

The language of science is filled with impersonal terms—numbers, variables, hypotheses, scientific laws, and so on—and problems formulated in the language of science are typically built on such concepts. Human concerns, on the other hand, are expressed with words like trust, caring, hope, love, optimism; and the strongest of these terms are reserved for the language of ethics—injustice and moral outrage.

The case of Intel, which we discussed in chapter 2, is an especially significant illustration of the importance of the language we use to formulate a problem. It demonstrates how serious a problem can become when a technical formulation of an important problem (that is, the Scientific/Technical perspective of Figure 4-3) takes precedence over ethical and spiritual concerns (that is, the Existential perspective).

Product liability and safety cases are almost always outstanding examples of this category of E_3. Another good example is the rights of smokers. Since these rights are framed in abstract, legal terms guaranteed by the U.S. Constitution (the Technical perspective), the ethical and moral responsibilities of tobacco manufacturers are conveniently side-stepped (the Existential perspective).

The issue of movie/television violence is not only another good example but one worth examining in detail. It is pertinent because its business and social aspects are virtually inseparable and because the battle is over the fundamental definition of the issue. The various sides in the debate interpret the Scientific/Technical perspective differently because they have different underlying ethical assumptions, based on both their Existential and Interpersonal/Social perspectives.

Phrasing the Movie/Television Violence Debate in Technical Language

A thirty-year, uninterrupted stream of research studies in the social sciences has shown consistently that there is a *nonnegligible, persistent correlation* between the exposure of children to movie/television violence and their heightened aggressiveness.[3] True, the correlations are not high, typically in the range of 0.2 to 0.3, but they are not zero. And yet, with very few exceptions, the movie/television industry has rejected almost *any* association between the exposure of children to movie/television violence and the increase in real-world violence or the heightened aggressiveness of children.

In rejecting the association, the movie/television industry and various social critics have responded with three technical objections to the research.[4] The first objection is to any *causal* link between movie/television violence and increased real-world violence or aggressiveness. The second is that other societal factors, such as the general violence in U.S. society, the breakdown of the family, and the easy availability of guns, *are more responsible* for societal violence than the movie/television industry is. In other words, they define the problem so that it belongs to someone else, who is more responsible than they are. The third technical objection is a constitutional objection (free speech).

It is true that strictly speaking there is no direct, causal connection between movie/television violence and real-world violence. This is because in today's Systems Age, there are few, if any, direct, causal connections between any two isolated events or phenomena. Thus, the movie/television industry is right about the lack of causality, but its reasons are wrong! The movie/television industry can't even get the Scientific/Technical perspective on the problem right.

No direct, causal connection can be proven because causality is applicable only in the simple world of the Machine Age. For instance, it is true that a cue stick is the *direct cause* of a cue ball slamming into another ball, and the movement of the second ball is the *end effect*. But such a simple situation is not the norm in a complex world filled with multiple causes and effects. It is also true that societal factors other than movie/television violence are more responsible for real-world violence. But this does not mean that movie/television violence is *not even a partial contributing factor* to real-world violence.

Existential concerns, spirituality, and recovery are central to organizations, not peripheral or secondary.

Notice that in this case, E_3 is fundamentally due to the inappropriate application of a Machine Age concept, causality, to a Systems Age issue. For this reason alone, the issue of movie/television violence is instructive and important to analyze. Indeed, we could say that it is in the direct interest of the movie/television industry to *deliberately commit* this E_3, since it suits both its business and political purposes. The industry is deliberately committing an E_3 when it criticizes the various social science studies for not establishing causality, when they could not and do not purport to do so in the first place! In effect, the industry is accusing the social sciences of solving the wrong problem and therefore rejects the solutions recommended. And the rejection is all based on the use of a single, technical word, *cause*.

Phrasing the Movie/Television Violence Debate in Ethical Language

The movie/television industry has chosen to adopt a predominantly technical phrasing of the problem because it wishes to avoid ethical and moral responsibilities. In doing so, however, it actually makes use of a very clever ethical argument, which to my knowledge, has never been stated explicitly.

THE ETHICS ARGUMENT

Whenever the relationship (correlation) between some phenomenon in the real world (for example, societal violence) and a simulation of that phenomenon by an industry (for example, movie/television violence) is substantially less than perfect, then the industry in question is warranted in doing nothing about it; indeed, it *ought not* do anything about it.

The following definition of the problem is implicit in the preceding argument:

THE IMPLICIT DEFINITION OF THE PROBLEM

Whenever the relationship (correlation) between some phenomenon in the real world (for example, societal violence) and a simulation of that phenomenon by an industry (for example, movie/television violence) is substantially less than perfect, then *no problem exists for the industry.* In order for a problem to exist for the industry, it has to exceed some threshold.

The preceding illustrates the importance of examining the interplay between arguments and the definitions of problems. The connection is so close that the separation between them is artificial at best. At worst, it is seriously misleading. The underlying arguments are important to bring to the surface because they contain the implicit assumptions we make about a situation.

Framing the issue in ethical terms allows us to analyze it explicitly from the vantage point of different ethical theories. For example, we can consider the differences between a utilitarian and a Kantian ethical analysis of the situation and the different formulations to which they lead.

From a strictly utilitarian, or cost-benefit perspective, the Ethics Argument and the Implicit Definition of the Problem have some validity. In a utilitarian ethical analysis, the problem is framed in terms of the benefits versus the costs of a proposed action. If the benefits to the movie/television industry of its actions, as measured in dollars alone, are great, and the corresponding costs, also measured in dollars, are low, then the industry is entitled, by this type of reasoning, to neglect the costs of its actions to the larger society. For this very reason, I have never been a fan of utilitarianism.

From the perspective of a Kantian ethical analysis, however, the whole tenor of the Ethics Argument changes drastically. The great German philosopher Immanuel Kant argued that we are ethically obligated to do as much as possible to improve the general welfare of society, *no matter how small the correlation* between our industry and real-world effects. Even if—indeed, especially if—the correlation were as low as 0.00001 between movie/television violence and real-world violence, the industry would still be obligated to act on behalf of humanity. To be sure, this imposes a severe condition—one that is more severe than the establishment of causality—but then this is precisely what Kantian ethics imposes on us. Thus, to be ethical is not to do what is easy or prudent, but rather what is difficult, and for this reason, controversial.

Whereas the utilitarian perspective raises the *ethics threshold* as high as possible, the Kantian perspective lowers it as much as possible. A Kantian perspective considers the very notion of an ethics threshold absolutely absurd. From a Kantian standpoint, it makes no sense to figure how much evil can be traded off in pursuit of good. Merely to think this way is unethical.

I can well imagine Kant's response to the movie/television industry's version of the Ethics Argument:

> This whole manner of thinking is an example of a poor ethical principle that pretends to apply in all situations, but surely does not, because a person who wishes to escape ethical responsibility can make the threshold as high as possible. Thus my dictum is "So act as to make the threshold as low as possible so that humankind will always err on the side of ethical responsibility."

From the standpoint of ethics, E_3 consists of choosing the wrong ethical formulation of a problem. In saying this, I need to emphasize once again that I am not saying that I or anyone else has a monopoly on truth or righteousness. Rather, I am saying that the formulation of a problem is not, and never can be, a purely impersonal, technical procedure. Problem formulation always has strong ethical and moral undertones. As a result, one of the best aids to problem formulation is bringing our underlying ethical assumptions up to the surface for explicit analysis.[5]

Lesson Number Five: Examine carefully every formulation of a problem for the implicit ethics threshold it contains; examine carefully how the formulation and the solution change depending on whether the threshold is made high or low.

Can Organizations Learn to Avoid E_3s?

Just because the concept of E_3 pertains to failures, that is, the explicit *commission* of errors, it is a grave mistake to think that there are no positive examples of organizations that have avoided E$_3$s. In many cases, however, this avoidance was due to luck, not to a systematic process.

For example, in one case, the executive committee of a major bank was given a financial analysis of a potential loan indicating that it was a highly desirable risk. For this reason, the entire committee was strongly predisposed to grant the loan.

However, something didn't seem right to one of the members of the committee. At the last second, he asked the seemingly innocuous question, "By the way, what's the business?" One of the other members flipped through a series of pages to finally locate the nature of the business. He was shocked to find that it was legal pornography (that is, it did not involve child pornography or other crimes).

On hearing the true nature of the business, the entire committee was shocked and stunned. Collectively they determined that there was no way they could grant the loan, even though every business indicator was positive, because it was not a business venture with which they wished to be associated. In turning down the loan request, they asked themselves the following question, "Do we wish to be known as 'the Porn Bank'?" The resounding answer was, "No!"

Human concerns are expressed with words like trust, caring, hope, love, optimism; the strongest of these terms are reserved for the language of ethics—injustice and moral outrage.

This seemingly simple example shows how crucial the formulation of a problem is. When the committee members looked at the loan in purely economic terms, they were willing to grant it. However, when they looked at the loan's broader systemic and social implications, it became clear that they should not grant it because of the negative publicity and the serious damage it would do to the ethical reputation of the bank.

What is most disturbing about the loan problem? It is the fact that, because of the nature of the loan-granting process, the ethical branch of the decision tree was almost overlooked entirely. It was only *by chance* that someone happened to ask about the nature of the business. This fundamental question should not have been left to chance. If the bank learned anything from this situation, it should have learned how important it is to incorporate seemingly innocuous questions into every potential loan. Even if (indeed, especially if) a loan makes sense financially, it may not make sense from the standpoint of negative publicity. Who would want to see their company appear on the front page of the *Wall Street Journal* or in the lead story on the six o'clock news identified as the Porn Bank or some other unsavory label?

Consider another example: Major fast-food organizations constantly distribute prizes to children. Most often, these take the form of various promotional toys. In deciding to distribute a toy or not, the organization carefully checks whether the toy can harm young children. However, even though a toy may satisfy the stringent safety procedures of well-qualified research and development laboratories, one cannot assume that it will be manufactured to the same safety requirements. Unfortunately, this happens to major fast-food organizations regularly.

In this particular example, the director of security for a major fast-food organization just happened to be walking by the executive offices one day. Two senior executives were frantically debating whether a certain set of promotional toys should be recalled or not. Apparently, two cases had already been reported where young children had ingested parts of the toys, which had lodged in their windpipes and could have caused asphyxiation. Fortunately, in both cases, the children were rushed to the emergency rooms of local hospitals and the toys were removed successfully.

In effect, the executives were asking, "How many more such cases have to occur before we will order a nationwide recall of the products from our sites?" On hearing this, the director of security raised the following questions: "How many more cases have to occur? Are we crazy? Isn't one case already one too many? Do we want it to be known that we were even considering such questions? There is no doubt in my mind whatsoever that we need to withdraw all of these toys immediately."

Notice that the security director's argument is an argument for lowering the threshold of ethical action as low as possible (withdrawing the toys). Also notice that whether we agree with the security director or not, the raising of such critical questions cannot be left to chance. It must be built in as an integral part of the problem-solving processes of organizations. In this particular case, the security director lobbied successfully to build in such questions as a fundamental part of the review process.

Conclusion

I can think of no better summary of the ideas in this chapter than the simple but profound words of Thomas Moore:

> In recent decades our language has become brittle and abstract. We use abbreviations as though they were words, we use a common jargon for our subtle emotional experiences, and we prefer tables, graphs, numbers, and step-by-step procedures

over lengthy reflection. All of this is the result of the spirited bias of the times. But the soul takes in things slowly and piecemeal, savoring the details and the qualities of expression. A good phrase may inspire meditation for many years, and a good tune may stay with us for a lifetime.

It makes a difference what kind of language we use to express our feelings and thoughts. Some words are more evocative than others, some fresher than those that immediately come to mind. Choosing the right word may make all the difference, and that choice requires art.[6]

Critical Questions for You and Your Organization

1. Which disciplines (for example, engineering, economics, law, human resource management, political science, and so on) exert a dominant influence over you or your organization's definition of critical problems? Which variables tend to predominate in your definitions?

2. Select a critical problem that has been formulated primarily from the vantage point of one discipline. Pick a diametrically opposite discipline from which to reformulate the problem. For instance, if you have formulated a problem primarily in terms of a technical discipline, then pick a human or social discipline in which to reformulate the problem. How do the solutions differ?

3. Do you and your organization explicitly formulate problems in ethical terms? Do you use one type of ethical formulation (utilitarian, Kantian) more than others? Why?

CHAPTER 6

Expanding the Boundaries of Problems

RATIONAL, adj. Devoid of all delusions save those of observation, experience, and reflection.
　　　—Ambrose Bierce,
　　　　The Devil's Dictionary

SOMETIME DURING THE 1950S, the world passed over a great divide: it moved from the Machine Age to the Systems Age. Although at the time few were aware of this important transition, today, all of us are struggling to understand and come to grips with it. The movement from the Machine Age to the Systems Age influences every aspect of our lives.

The fourth and fifth categories of E_3 are both due to the failure to think systemically and, more generally, the failure to understand the Systems Age that we live in. Both the fourth category, drawing the boundaries or scope of a problem too narrowly, and the fifth category, ignoring the system or broader context in which all problems are imbedded, are best discussed within the context of how complex systems work. This, in turn, requires an understanding of how, and why, virtually everything in today's world is highly interconnected, which in turn requires that we understand the differences between Machine Age thinking and Systems Age thinking.

Bounded Thinking Equals Machine Age Thinking

The following fundamental assumption underlies many of the current approaches to the design and management of organizations and societal institutions today:[1]

> The problems facing organizations, institutions, and whole societies are bounded; they are limited in scope and magnitude. Therefore, simple solutions are not only appropriate but suffice: for every complex problem, there is both a simple formulation and a simple solution.

There is no question that if it is possible to bound a problem or situation, a manager's life becomes much easier. He or she only need consider a simple and restricted set of problems and solutions.

Bounding as a tactic for solving problems was appropriate in the Machine Age, the age of the Industrial Revolution, roughly from the 1700s to the mid-1950s. Problems then were largely reduced in their scope and magnitude. Most problems were also independent of one another and could be solved in isolation. This no longer applies; indeed, in today's world, bounded thinking creates fertile ground for E_3.

The Ultimate Driving Machine?

BMW is commonly advertised as the Ultimate Driving Machine. A more accurate portrayal would be the Ultimate Driving *System,* for a modern BMW is not a simple machine; it functions as a total system, and the differences are profound.

In a modern BMW—as in any modern luxury car—the different parts not only communicate with one another constantly but also change their properties in relationship to one another as conditions change. For example, a modern luxury car can change the stiffness of its springs, shock absorbers, and steering mechanism depending on road conditions. This is made possible by a mini on-board computer that constantly monitors the behavior and performance of the car as a total system. This idea has progressed to the point where new motor oils have been developed that change their molecular properties as driving conditions change!

Performance comparisons of a BMW M3 offer a powerful illustration of the fact that this car is a system. The M3 often finishes near the middle when compared to other cars in tests of its separate features, for example, acceleration time from 0 to 60 miles per hour. Yet from the standpoint of total driving performance, an M3 consistently finishes first or near the top compared to other cars in its class.

In contrast to a luxury car system, the parts of a machine typically do not change their properties in response to one another. The parts are not only relatively fixed and stable, but also they are independent of one another. If a part of a machine fails, it can generally be pulled out and an identical replacement part substituted. On the other hand, if a system fails, the failure generally cannot be located in a single defective part. Rather, the failure is typically a failure of the whole, or a larger subassembly, for example, the whole braking system in a modern automobile.

Are Organizations Machines?

In the world of organizations, while most have become complex systems, we still persist in designing and managing them as though they were simple machines. This misunderstanding is so fundamental that it is almost singly responsible for the mess that the vast majority of businesses are in today. Even more frustrating is the reality that many of the very organizations whose products are responsible for the transition from the Machine Age to the Systems Age, for example, computers and telecommunications equipment, are themselves dominated by Machine Age thinking. As Alvin Toffler has observed:

Most American managers still think of [an] organization

In the world of organizations, while most have become complex systems, we still persist in designing and managing them as though they were simple machines. This misunderstanding is so fundamental that it is almost singly responsible for the mess that the vast majority of businesses are in today.

as a "machine" whose parts can be tightened or loosened, "tuned up," or lubricated. This is the basic bureaucratic metaphor . . .[2]

An example of Machine Age thinking is the tendency of American firms, until very recently, to identify the factors compromising quality by looking solely within the four walls of their plants and facilities. They bounded the problem of quality by only looking for and attempting to eliminate the sources of defects that lay within their manufacturing processes and the confines of their facilities.

Japanese firms, on the other hand, typically take a much broader view of the entire system within which their plants and facilities function. They have a history of looking at the forces that pose threats to quality from both inside and outside, which means that they carefully monitor the quality of materials and parts provided by their suppliers in addition to the processes within their facilities. They attempt to understand the manufacturing processes of their suppliers. From a Japanese firm's perspective, the proper unit of analysis is not the individual plant or facility, it is the plant plus the broader system in which it exists and functions.

This does not mean that Japanese firms, or the entire Japanese manufacturing system, are thereby superior in all respects. No society is free, and hence unbounded, in all important aspects. The Japanese, for instance, are bounded by their culture, history, and geography. This often prevents them from understanding and hence interacting effectively with other cultures.

Bounded Systems Thinking

In spite of all the talk in recent years about systems thinking, as reflected, for example, in popular books such as *The Fifth Discipline* and *Re-engineering the Corporation,* we still do not have truly comprehensive and systematic approaches to systems thinking.[3]

We are just beginning to realize that a much larger number of dimensions must be considered in the design and the operation of all organizations. In addition, every one of the dimensions themselves must be considered in a broader vein.

The major defect in most current approaches to systems thinking is that the approaches themselves are bounded! Most of the approaches are primarily cognitive and intellectual; they deal with the Scientific/Technical dimensions of problems. They conceive of organizations primarily as abstract systems that merely pass information, raw materials, or finished products between their various parts or departments. Such approaches are

inherently defective because they do not take into account the broader purposes and needs of people and organizations. They ignore the fact that people have deep emotional, ethical, and even spiritual needs. They ignore the
Interpersonal/Social and Existential dimensions.

Emotional, ethical, and spiritual impulses are among the strongest
impulses that humans have. And yet, for the most part, these issues are
excluded from the literature of systems and organizations. But no purely
cognitive or intellectual approach to improving organizations—in essence,
no idea, no matter how logical—can succeed without the deep emotional,
ethical, and even spiritual buy-in of the members of an organization.

Why then have such impulses or aspects been ignored? Because the
basic concept of a machine, from which, ironically, most systems
approaches are derived, exclude feelings and spirituality. By definition, a
machine has no feelings, no spirit, no will. It runs according to laws that
are essentially deterministic and mechanical. This, unfortunately, is what
most approaches to systems thinking have inherited without their full
awareness.

Thinking Systemically

E_3 arises fundamentally because of the failure to think and to act systemically. The situation that Sears found itself in a couple of years ago is a
textbook case of this failure. In an attempt to reverse its financial losses (an
"initial crisis"), Sears instituted a bonus plan. Its intent was to bring more
business into its auto repair facilities by rewarding employees. The more
business they brought in, the greater the bonus. The plan worked all right,
but not in the ways that Sears executives intended.

Employees increased business by recommending unnecessary auto
repairs. In a number of cases, customers were bilked for large amounts of
money. When word got out, Sears faced a crisis worse than the original one,
namely, damage to its venerable reputation.

Although Sears recovered from this crisis, the organization paid a
high price. Following are some key lessons concerning what it means for
an organization to think systemically in order to avoid such crises:

1. No proposed solution to any corporate or societal problem should
   be undertaken without first examining its impacts on the total
   system.

2. The more desirable a proposed solution or argument appears, the

more questions one should ask and the more suspicious one should be of adopting it.

3. Unless a proposed solution to a problem or crisis is examined in the context of the total system in which it will function, it may lead to a worse problem or crisis.

4. In examining the effects of any argument or solution, one must look at not only its structural (for example, financial) effects, but also its emotional, cultural, and symbolic (for example, reputational) effects. In other words, what good does it do to empower employees if it merely exacerbates the latent defects inherent in a dysfunctional system?

The Old Bounded World

The Machine Age rested on a small number of fundamental assumptions or rules:

- The world is bounded sharply in space and time.
- The world is predictable and stable.
- All things can be decomposed into independent atoms.
- Analysis is the method for gaining true knowledge of all things.
- Knowledge itself can be subdivided into autonomous branches or disciplines.
- The various branches of knowledge can be arrayed hierarchically; that is, some branches are more fundamental than others.

For hundreds, even thousands, of years, the majority of humans lived and worked only a few miles from their place of birth. The limits of the world were the distances a person could travel on foot or by horseback in a few days. The basic unit of social life was the immediate family, clan, tribe, or village. Identification with a city, state, or nation came only recently. To say that life was confined is putting it mildly. It was clearly and sharply *bounded* in space (locale), time (horizon), and livelihood (occupation and social class).[4]

Today's Unbounded World

Humankind today is besieged by a multitude of social units, each vying for loyalty. Through unparalleled social upheaval, we are each potential members of a multitude of family and institutional arrangements, often simultaneously. The traditional family, clan, village, city, state, and even nation face previously unheard of challenges and threats to identity and existence. Traditional social and economic units are being replaced by regional economic trading blocks, multinational corporations and institutions, defense alliances, and on and on.

Technology in general, and television in particular, has altered our lives profoundly in ways we are just beginning to comprehend.[5] Technology has invaded the once "back-stage," private lives of persons and institutions to such a degree that, for all practical purposes, everything is now "up front and personal" for all the world to see. As a result, there are no secrets in the strict sense anymore because there are no hard boundaries anymore.

Consider once again the case of Rodney King, the motorist who was beaten severely by the Los Angeles police. One of the most important aspects of this case has received virtually no attention: the widespread purchase of camcorders by ordinary citizens has turned everyone into potential investigative reporters. The invention and distribution of camcorders has not only allowed people to record pictures of their personal friends and families, but it has also allowed them to record events once open only to professional photographers, news reporters, documentary film makers, and so on. Thus, how the police once behaved "back stage" in the relative comfort, security, and privacy (bounded space) of their station houses, or on isolated streets, is no longer exempt from widespread public scrutiny. Back-stage events (private space) have now become front-stage revelations. Indeed, they are now the subject of prime-time news shows around the world.

If an event is dramatic enough, it can become news anywhere and everywhere. In addition, events that happen anywhere can affect other seemingly unrelated events around the world. Chernobyl is a perfect illustration. It took about two weeks for the cloud of radiation from Chernobyl to encircle the globe and physically contaminate the salmon off the coast of the state of Washington. It took less than half a day, however, for the grain markets in Chicago to react. If the breadbasket of the former Soviet Union was to be knocked out of commission for a hundred years due to the dangerous radiation released by Chernobyl, then the market for future grain prices in Chicago would be affected dramatically; "business time" is now free from the moorings of "physical time."

Today, the world is so interconnected in space and time that any event around the globe can potentially affect other events in ways of which we are only dimly aware. Thus, the old, long-held assumption of a world sharply bounded in space and time no longer holds. In light of this fundamental alteration of ordinary space and time, as well as the sheer uncertainty of knowing which improbable events out of thousands will connect to affect our lives, organizations, and world, how do we manage institutions?

Some thirty years ago, Alvin Toffler astutely observed that we were suffering from "future shock," a phrase he introduced into the language.[6] Essentially, future shock is the growing inability to function normally because of the rapid speedup and highly stressful overload of events. What Toffler did not foresee, and is thus still unable to explain even in his most recent book, *Power Shift*, is that future shock is itself being exacerbated by a complementary complicating force, which can be called *Boundary Shock*. As a result, the effects on people that he foresaw are even more intense.

Systems: A Series of Linkages

The following three examples illustrate the failure to think systemically. Each of them is also a prime example of E_3.

Electronic Funds Transfer

In New York City, the electronic transfer of huge sums of money between financial institutions is an everyday occurrence. The executives of one large bank bragged about the security of their computer system, which transferred over $1.5 billion every working day. Upon hearing this, a consultant bet he could crack the system in less than a day. The consultant and his colleagues noted that while the computer part of the system was well protected—difficult-to-crack codes made it nearly impossible for unauthorized persons to gain access—the rest of the system was highly vulnerable.

In order for other institutions to receive transferred funds, they had to have access to codes. The codes were delivered every day by a lone courier on a moped who traveled across Manhattan from the bank to the various receiving institutions. One of the consultant's colleagues struck up a conversation with the courier and after a short while asked him how much money it would take for the courier to reveal the codes. The answer was $100,000.

While to the average person this is a large sum of money, to the bank it was approximately 0.000002 of one percent of the annual amount of funds transferred! Given that the courier only made $22,000 per year, it would have been literally unthinkable to propose to the bank's executives that the courier make $100,000 annually. And yet, the security of a $1.5 billion-per-day operation depended upon a $22,000 link in the system!

The point should be clear: what good does it do to have the best computer system in the world (Scientific/Technical solution) if it can be compromised by a weak human link in the chain (Social problem)? Solving the problem of how to build the best computer system is the solution to the wrong problem. The right problem is how to design the best combined computer *and* human system.

AT&T

A few years ago, a brownout occurred in New York City due to an overload on the ConEd power system. Because AT&T is dependent upon ConEd to provide the power to run its electronic communication systems, it experienced a breakdown. Two of the AT&T systems that depend on ConEd are extremely critical; they provide the information for the air traffic control systems that manage planes in and out of La Guardia and Kennedy airports. When the brownout occurred, the power to AT&T's system dropped. A backup generator automatically kicked in. As is so often the case with complex systems, however, the generator failed. Fortunately, there was a backup to the backup in the form of a forty-eight-volt battery with a six-hour life.

As soon as the battery kicked in, an alarm sounded to alert a human operator to monitor the life of the battery. Before six hours elapsed, the battery had to be replaced. Unfortunately, in this particular case, no human operators were available to hear the alarm. By the time someone did hear it, six and a half hours had elapsed and airplanes were circling dangerously in the air because the computer systems to bring them down safely were not functioning.

The irony and tragedy of this whole situation is this: the operators were not available to hear the alarm because they were attending a class on a new backup system!

Once again, the point should be clear: what good is the best technology in the world if the humans who manage it are not factored in as integral parts of the whole system?

Dow Corning

Silicon breast implants accounted for only 1 percent of Dow Corning's

Emotional, ethical, and spiritual impulses are among the strongest impulses that humans have. And yet, for the most part, these issues are excluded from the literature of systems and organizations.

total profits. According to one of the conventional tools of risk manage-ment, the resultant risk to Dow Corning's total business should therefore have been at most 0.01 times Dow Corning's total profits. The unfavorable publicity that resulted from women suing Dow Corning for illnesses they claimed were due to implants was, however, responsible for a 22 percent drop in total profits. Furthermore, even though conventional science has failed to demonstrate any substantial link between breast implants and the symptoms experienced by women, the impending lawsuits threaten nonetheless to bankrupt one of the most powerful corporations in the world, Dow Chemical, which owns 50 percent of Dow Corning.

All three of the preceding examples demonstrate that systems are composed of elements that are linked together in complex ways. What is tragic is that often the most obvious linkages are overlooked. No one is viewing the system as a set of integrated components that are highly depen-dent on one another. When this interdependence is realized, we have the starting point for systems thinking.

The Systems Age: A Tale of Two Companies

Once upon a time, there were two companies, M and S. They both started out around the same time, had equivalent early histories, and were organized and run in the same manner. Over time, however, their philoso-phies of business and ways of operating became radically different.

Machine Age Limited

M, or Machine Age Limited, was the epitome of a traditional, old-line business. It was a success from day one of its founding early in the twenti-eth century. Indeed, it seemed as if M could do no wrong. The market not only grabbed up whatever M produced, but it made M the market leader.

M was organized and run like a machine. Different businesses were conducted by independent business units that had virtually no contact with one another. M was a machine not only because its various parts existed independently of one another but also because they functioned independently. Thus, the success of business X, which produced widgets, didn't depend on the success of business Y, which produced gidgets. X and Y rose and fell on their own individual merits.

Each unit not only had its own separate accounting, finance, market-ing, and production departments, but there was little communication between them. A major, implicit assumption was this: all problems can be broken down into their separate accounting, finance, and so on components. The only entities that the separate business units shared were M's corporate legal and public relations departments and senior management of the corporation.

For a long, long time—far into the twentieth century—this way of running a business proved enormously successful for M and all the other companies that adopted this model. Beginning around 1950, however, something started to change. Crude, cheap imitations of M's products began appearing from abroad and even from home. Because the first imitations were so bad, and further because M had dominated its home markets for so long, M not only dismissed the first imitations with disdain and arrogance but acted as if it could dismiss anything its new competitors would ever produce. What M didn't see, and perhaps couldn't because the pattern was slow in forming and hence imperceptible, was that the first crude imitations were merely the toeholds of an invasion that was taking shape. In what seemed like no time at all—a bare ten to fifteen years—the first crude imitations became more than threats; they became major market leaders in their own right.

All during this time, M was lulled into complacency. It didn't spend the money it should have on research and development: developing new products and improving old ones. In addition, M didn't really experiment with or take seriously the new models for restructuring companies that were being pioneered in other cultures around the world.

When the day finally came that M's back was up against the wall, it reacted in a knee-jerk fashion. Individual business units were cut back indiscriminately. Downsizing became the buzzword of the day. This was soon followed by one management gimmick and quick fix after another.

No matter what M did, the situation only spiraled downward. For instance, exactly one year after M initiated a major downsizing and restructuring initiative, its bottom line was even worse. Morale was at an all-time low. Absenteeism and labor disputes were at an all-time high. Everyone feared that he or she would be the next to be fired. In addition, all the employees were fatigued because they were overworked, which contributed to the further deterioration of the quality of M's products and services, which in turn caused profits to dip even more. Accidents and outbursts of violence not only became commonplace but also increased dramatically. M was in a total state of panic, even crisis. It seemed as if it might go out of business or be taken over. Possibilities that were once unthinkable were now all too real.

Systems Age, Inc.

The early history and behavior of S, which stands for Systems Age, Inc., were essentially identical to those of M. S faced the same set of circumstances that M did, and in the beginning, it reacted just like M. It was organized into separate business units. During the 1950s, it faced the same set of problems as well. Like M, it ignored and denied the threats that appeared in the market. It closed ranks and pretended that things would return to normal, which of course never happened.

Something gnawed at S's CEO, however. If only vaguely, he sensed that something was wrong precisely because he couldn't say exactly what it was. Unlike M's CEO, he began to notice that strange things he couldn't explain were happening. Business units that were in theory supposed to be independent of one another were not in reality. Threats to one of his company's business units were affecting other units. Threats to one of S's products were spreading to other products as well. Something was happening that affected the whole of S. Worst of all, the things that were happening seemed beyond anyone's control.

S's CEO began asking himself uncomfortable and troubling questions such as, "If we were starting S today, would we create it in the same way? What if we no longer know our business as we think we do?"

Instead of dismissing these questions because he couldn't answer them, as many of his fellow CEOs were prone to do (if they even raised them in the first place), S's CEO called in his top executives and put before them the questions he had asked himself. He also asked some additional questions that were just as difficult, and even more threatening: "Are we the right persons to lead S if S has to change drastically in order to survive? If we aren't, who is? And what does 'right' mean anyway?"

S's top executives did not greet their boss's questions with enthusiasm. If anything, they tried to talk him out of even raising them, let alone pursuing them. In their view, why be a worrywart when things were still okay? The few disturbing signs were only minor.[7]

S's CEO was not easily dissuaded. He stated bluntly,

> Until we can prove the case either way, I will not be satisfied, and none of you should be either. I've made a decision. All of us need to go back to school. I don't mean that we need to enroll in formal degree programs. Instead, I've decided that once a month for the next year and a half we are going to bring in speakers from the academic world, from government, from

other industries, and from nonprofit organizations. They'll
share with us what changes they see occurring and their theories
as to why such changes are occurring. I don't intend these to be
one-sided lectures or conversations. I want outsiders who can
summarize and speak effectively without jargon about what they
see happening, and even what they think will happen, whether
it is pure speculation or not. All that I'm asking of each of you at
this point is that you keep an open mind. If by the end of six
months we feel that this is a waste of time, then we'll stop it.

Even though S's CEO said he would stop the program at the end of
the first six months if the group agreed that it was not valuable, uncon-
sciously he had already made the decision that S was going to change fundamentally. And there was going to be a sorting out process with regard to
who was best suited to manage the new S. In sum, not every one of his current staff would remain. It was even up in the air whether he himself would
be right for the new organization.

After the first six speakers, it was clear to S's CEO that significant
structural change was already afoot around the globe that was going to alter
substantially the way business was conducted. Although none of the speakers could spell out precisely the forces responsible for the change, the CEO
concluded that the exercise had nonetheless proven invaluable. Because
none of the speakers could be precise, however, his immediate staff was
split down the middle regarding the benefits. Those opposed to the exercise said it was of little benefit since none of the speakers could pinpoint
precisely what was happening and why. Those who were in favor of continuing argued that the exercise was a benefit for two reasons. First, it was
giving them important insights, which, while they couldn't relate them
directly to their day-to-day duties and responsibilities, were still valuable.
They felt stretched by the program. This in itself was of value. Second, the
fact that none of the speakers could settle the question about whether significant changes were afoot that would substantially alter their business
was, in itself, reason for continuing the exercise until the situation became
clear. What could they lose in the process?

One of the most significant sessions took place near the end of the
first year. The speaker shared with them her experiments with a variety of
organizations in different industries that were going through a fundamental redesign. She outlined a method whereby many of an organization's
stakeholders could participate in its redesign in order to make it continu-

ally adaptive to whatever changes occurred.[8] The method was explicitly designed to raise to the surface unconscious and taken-for-granted assumptions that an organization was making about itself, its industry, and its surrounding environment.[9] Once an organization's assumptions were out in the open, participants were given permission to challenge each and every one of them. They were also given permission to redesign the organization's entire structure in order to come up with new structures that not only could live in whatever new environments arose but also could prosper. The speaker pointed out that to take full advantage of the method, everyone connected with the organization would have to go back to school. They had to gain new knowledge so they could be full participants in the reinvention of their organization. The speaker also stressed that the organization's top executive staff would have to tolerate some outrageous, and even threatening, proposals, such as redoing its entire reward and compensation systems. For instance, some organizations were contemplating taking across-the-board pay cuts instead of letting people go during hard times. The speaker stressed that everyone had to be prepared to tolerate such ideas, as outrageous as they might be, if the process was to work.

E_3 arises fundamentally because of the failure to think and to act systemically.

Above all, the speaker pointed out that the world was going through a transition—more accurately, a revolution—at least as profound as the shift from the Agrarian to the Industrial Age. Now, however, the world was shifting from the Machine Age to the Systems Age.[10] In the Machine Age—the world in which the vast majority of organizations were born, including S—everything could be neatly divided into separate, self-standing entities. For instance, complex business problems could be broken down into separate areas such as product design, finance, operations, distribution, and so on. In this world, there was little or no crossover between separate business functions, business units, or geographical regions. Everything was neatly compartmentalized. All of this, however, was becoming passé, if not dangerously out of touch with the profoundly changing nature of the world. Things were becoming increasingly intertwined in complex and mysterious ways.

More and more organizations were finding that if they didn't get products right the first time out, they wouldn't be around to get them right subsequently. But this meant that the design, production, marketing, and finance people had to work together not only as a team but also as a tightly knit system. They had to do more than share ideas and information. They had to integrate ideas and information if they were going to build products that customers wanted, that were cost efficient to manufacture and sell, and that were attractive and of high quality.

Mess Management

Most of all, she stressed that the organizations of the Machine Age were built on a defunct paradigm. The parts of an organization were no longer self-standing or self-sufficient entities. They were tightly coupled. All problems were interconnected. Since the English language had no single word for a whole series of interconnected problems, she had to appropriate one: *mess.*[11] As a result, all organizations were in the business of managing messes or Mess Management.

Although it was stated clearly and with a minimum of jargon, most of what the speaker said went over, or through, the majority of the minds, hearts, and souls of S's top executives. In a word, minds, hearts, and souls that had been shaped by the Machine Age couldn't make the transition to the Systems Age. The words and the concepts just didn't compute, no matter how many examples the speaker gave, how patient she was, or even how persistent. S's CEO got the message, however. He was convinced that something major was afoot.

Downsizing: A Machine Age Tactic

Although the previous stories are caricatures, the differences between the two types of organizations are real. Far too many of our industrial giants—the GMs, IBMs, and Searses of the world—unfortunately fit the M model. They have put off making fundamental changes until it is almost too late. Or they have engaged in short-term quick fixes, such as downsizing, which are not fully appropriate to the nature of the problems and challenges they are facing.

Downsizing is one of the most powerful contemporary illustrations of solving the wrong problem precisely. As a result, it is a premiere example of *not* thinking systemically. For this very reason, it is a general indictment of the lack of leadership in corporate America. It is also a perfect illustration of how institutions and whole societies, and not merely individuals, are capable of committing E_3s.

Downsizing is not only a fad but also a reflex action that has spread like wildfire throughout corporate America. Everyone does it because everyone else does, and they don't know what else to do to cut costs and make organizations more efficient. It is, therefore, all the more remarkable that the arguments for downsizing have rarely been articulated clearly and systematically, let alone received the sustained criticism they deserve.[12] In effect, downsizing is akin to putting an anorexic on a diet.

The scorecard for downsizing is unequivocally negative.[13] Nine to twelve months after a major downsizing effort, the overwhelming majority of organizations are no better off, and some are even worse off. There are three primary reasons why.

First, the morale, spirit, and hope of those spared by downsizing are generally shattered. The result is a vicious downward spiraling of the organization. Those remaining are full of guilt because they were spared while so many of their friends and colleagues were fired. In addition to being overworked and stressed out, they live under a constant shadow of fear that they will eventually be let go as well. Such conditions are generally fatal to individual and organizational effectiveness, lowering the quality of output even further and exacerbating the very conditions that led to downsizing in the first place.

Second, the vast majority of downsizing efforts really do not cut costs. Many organizations have had to hire back, at significantly higher consulting rates, those who were let go. Often those who were terminated possessed critical information without which the organization found it difficult to function.

Third, downsizing is not a strategy for competitiveness in the Systems Age. By itself, downsizing does not address the critical question: What is the *structure* that our organization needs to be competitive in the new global marketplace?

Downsizing is a Machine Age tactic, and as we have emphasized repeatedly throughout this book, Machine Age tactics are generally ineffective in responding to Systems Age issues. Downsizing mainly affects one critical aspect of an organization—its size. Downsizing also affects, but does not directly address, whether the current structure of an organization is appropriate for its environment, for example, whether an organization has the appropriate number of departments, business functions, or business units, and whether the connections between departments, functions, and units are appropriate. When these issues are not addressed, downsizing may actually make things worse. Downsizing is not only the wrong solution to the wrong problem, it is a wrong solution that brings new and even worse problems in its wake.

In sum, downsizing defines the financial problems of an organization as due mainly to its size. This definition instructs us to solve the problems of organizational inefficiencies in terms of one variable and one variable alone, the size of an organization's work force. Downsizing typically does not define the problem as rooted in the larger system of an organization. As a consequence, downsizing is a compound form of E_3: first, it is a wrong definition of the problem because it focuses on a limited number of the wrong variables, and second, it creates new problems as a result of implementation of the wrong solution to the wrong problem.

Systems Age Alternatives

Fortunately, we do have a few examples of companies and individuals that understand the difference between Machine Age thinking and Systems Age thinking. Chaparral Steel is a good example of an S-type organization, and Ben Woodhouse of Dow Chemical Company provides a good example of thinking systemically to sell an idea.

A Systems Age Alternative to Downsizing

Today, the world is so interconnected in space and time that any event around the globe can potentially affect other events in ways of which we are only dimly aware.

All of Chaparral Steel's policies are designed to work together to improve the company as an entire system. The company understands that simple-minded strategies, such as indiscriminate cuts or downsizing, can bring on even worse problems. Thus, instead of downsizing in hard times, Chaparral has instituted policies designed to improve the morale of all employees. Laying people off is a last resort. Instead, everyone takes a pay cut, with top executives taking the biggest cut of all. The effect on morale, loyalty, and trust is incredible. The policy pays off by improving the effectiveness of the organization, which is especially needed in hard times.

Another Chaparral policy relates to education. At any one point in time, at least 80 percent of Chaparral Steel's employees are in school.[14] They are encouraged to constantly apply their education to the continual reinvention of the organization as a whole. They are rewarded for innovations that revolutionize the entire process of making steel. In other words, Chaparral defines its basic problem as the continual reinvention of the whole system. To this end, constant reeducation is one important part of the solution.

Selling Ideas in the Systems Age

Ben Woodhouse is the head of Global Issues Management for the Dow Chemical Company in Midland, Michigan. Ben and Dow Chemical were the first corporate sponsors of the University of Southern California Center for Crisis Management, which I founded in 1986 and directed until 1996. Ben not only bet on a new field, Crisis Management (CM), but he bet on it in its early stages of existence, when it did not have much going for it other than the promise of an obviously important idea.

Betting on CM in the early stages of its development is not the point of this story, however. The point is *how* Ben sold CM to his organization. This story is important to those of us who work in CM because people constantly ask us how to sell CM to organizations that don't see the need for it, which is, unfortunately, still a significant number.[15] But the story is more important as an illustration of how virtually any idea needs to be sold in today's world.

Ben's story is a textbook case of applying systems thinking to a problem. Ben knew instinctively that CM would be a multiple sell. He had to sell it repeatedly to multiple audiences both inside and outside of Dow Chemical over a span of five to seven years, before Dow as a whole would integrate it into daily operations.

To accomplish this, Ben constantly sold CM to his counterparts within Dow, that is, to executives at his level, to his counterparts at other chemical companies, and to others both up and down the corporate hierarchy. In addition, he got CM onto the agenda of the chemical industry's major trade association, the Chemical Manufacturing Association (CMA), and saw to it that CM became a top priority there as well. He helped get senior Dow executives to serve on key panels of the CMA to push and promote CM throughout the industry.

In this way, the need for CM at Dow constantly came in through multiple channels. Ben knew instinctively that the only successful strategy for selling CM would be a systemic strategy. Solving the problem of how to sell CM to one unit or person within Dow, no matter how well placed that unit or person, would be finding the right solution to the wrong problem. So Ben broadened the group of stakeholders to whom he attempted to sell CM in order to get Dow to buy it.

Lesson Number Six: Never believe that it is sufficient to sell an idea to a single individual (stakeholder), no matter how well placed he or she is within an organization. An important idea needs to be sold to the widest possible array of stakeholders because only if it is adopted by the whole system will it be successful.

Conclusion

Dow Chemical is a good example of the need for organizations to constantly learn and relearn the art of solving the right problems by thinking systemically. As of this writing, Dow has received a major legal judgment against it with regard to silicon breast implants. In the mind of Dow Chemical, Dow Corning was a separate joint venture between it and Corning for the purpose of manufacturing breast implants. In the minds of jurors, however, Dow Chemical was not separate, even though it owned "only 50 percent" of Dow Corning.

An organization is not truly systemic until it learns to think and to act systemically in *all* its operations.

Critical Questions for You and Your Organization

1. Make a list of three to five critical problems that either you or your organization failed to define in broad, systems terms. Why did this happen?

2. For each of the problems, what critical linkages were left out in the definitions of the problems? Were the linkages that were overlooked primarily Technical or Interpersonal/Social? What if anything can be done to rectify the situation in your organization?

3. Show how the culture of your organization contributes to the definition of important problems. That is, show the "linkages" between your organization's culture and the ways in which it typically defines problems.

CHAPTER 7

Managing the Paradoxes Inherent in Problems

[The boomerang principle] takes effect whenever one actor in an interdependent system attempts to act unilaterally, in ignorance or defiance of the other actors. At first, typically, the actor meets with resistance; his initiative throws the rest of the system out of balance, and the system fights back. Either the actors retaliate and the conflict escalates, or else they concede in unanticipated ways. Sometimes the system adjusts and endures; the initial actor may even gain from his assertion, though seldom precisely as he had intended. Often he loses. Sometimes the system collapses.

> —Robert B. Reich,
> *Tales of the New America*

The idea behind the chain of stores known as Incredible Universe is simple: bigger is better, and much bigger is much better. In the past four years these "gigastores" have sprouted up in the American exurban landscape, each boasting five football fields of retail space crammed with just about everything that could remotely be interpreted as "electronic."

Perhaps the managers at Tandy Corp., based in Fort Worth, Texas, should have heeded another aphorism: the bigger they come, the harder they fall. That describes roughly what happened last week when Tandy . . . acknowledged that Incredible Universe was really an incredible flop and pulled the plug on the entire 17-store operation. The closings, plus the store's losses, totaled some $230 million and completely wiped out Tandy's profits for 1996.

> —*Time* magazine

THE RULES OF BUSINESS have changed radically. If these changes were minor, then perhaps it would be easier for us to understand them and adapt to them. But the changes are not minor, and as a result not only have the old rules stopped working, but businesses that continue to play by the old rules may actually be making their problems worse. Understanding the old rules and why they no longer work is a task of fundamental importance, which we addressed in chapter 6. We also discussed the problems that arise when we apply bounded or Machine Age thinking in today's Systems Age, in which everything is interrelated. This chapter explores another characteristic of the Systems Age—paradox. We will look at the pervasiveness of paradox in our world today as well as some guidelines for managing it.

The Paradox of "Bigger Is Better"

One of the most interesting and subtle forms of E_3 involves decisions related to expansion. Whether we are talking about a bigger business, a bigger product, a bigger market, or a bigger nuclear weapon, "bigger is better" is a prime paradox of the Systems Age.

Most Western societies are preoccupied, if not obsessed, with bigness. In every sphere of human activity, bigger or more is believed to be better. And yet, as we shall see, this long-standing belief is becoming increasingly invalid. Understanding the paradox of bigness and the unintended effects of growth in the Systems Age is key to understanding why the old rules of doing business have collapsed.

The following story is a prime example of how the belief that "bigger is better" can backfire in today's business world. In September 1980, after a wave of unfavorable publicity, Proctor & Gamble (P&G) was forced to take its product, Rely tampons, off the market. According to *Fortune* magazine, "government researchers reported that over 70% of toxic-shock patients in one study had worn [the] single brand [Rely]," a fact strongly disputed by P&G's top scientists, which was also reported in *Fortune*.[1] Although Rely accounted for less than 1 percent of P&G's total annual sales of over $10 billion in 1980, P&G still took a $75 million loss on its Rely business and a reduction of $0.91 in its net earnings per share of $7.78.[2]

In a sense, toxic shock syndrome (TSS) is a result of our undying fascination with the "bigger is better" syndrome. As an August 1981 article in *Fortune* put it, the menstrual products industry got caught up in an "absorbency sweepstakes."[3] Each new innovation by one manufacturer spurred the others to match or exceed it. In addition, the innovations came at a time when women welcomed the freedom they gained by using slimmer pads and tampons that could remain in place for longer periods of time.

TSS hit at the height of the absorbency sweepstakes. It is interesting to note, however, that other than an observed association with tampons in general and with P&G's Rely in particular, there was no definitive proof that tampons "caused" TSS. The best thinking of the research community at the time was that a toxin produced by a bacterium, *Staphylococcus aureus,* was the underlying cause of TSS.[4] Researchers also seemed convinced that the bacteria in the TSS cases were a mutant strain. Because the tampons' greater absorbency allowed them to be left in a woman's body for a longer period of time, the new tampons were believed to give the bacteria a more fertile environment in which to grow. Another theory was that the tampons helped the infection along by irritating the lining of the vagina, thus giving the bacteria easier entry into the body's blood stream.[5]

Thus, the initial perceived advantage of "super" absorbency turned into a major disadvantage due to unintended side effects. As Edward Tenner shows in his recent book, *Why Things Bite Back: Technology and the Revenge of Unintended Consequences,* this is becoming a general phenomenon, occurring again and again. Products or events initially thought to be "good" turn out to have unintended "bad" effects.[6]

Why Bigger Is No Longer Necessarily Better

The arcane topic of nuclear weapons is, strangely enough, one of the very best examples to help us understand why bigger is no longer better in the Systems Age. The control of nuclear weapons is one of the paramount issues of the twentieth century; most issues, in fact, are dwarfed in comparison. And what we have learned in the struggle to control nuclear weapons illuminates some of the most profound changes in the world of business.

For over forty-five years, a horrendous arms race ensued between the United States and the former Soviet Union. Even after the two (then) superpowers already possessed enough weapons to destroy the other thousands of times over, the arsenals of both sides continued to proliferate at alarming rates. The more each side struggled to break free from the deadly embrace in which they were locked, the more each was drawn into the sickening nightmare of a potential nuclear confrontation that neither wanted. This was especially true as it became apparent that there would be no winners (good guys) in a nuclear war, only losers (bad guys).

Almost from their beginning, nuclear weapons were recognized as special. They did not obey the "logic" of traditional weapons or warfare. To use a highly simplified example, in an earlier century a nation with an army of ten thousand soldiers was generally superior to a nation with an army of one thousand soldiers, that is, bigger was better. Or, in slightly different words, *more* of something initially judged to be good (soldiers) would lead to *more* of an outcome also judged to be good (greater security). Conversely, *less* of something initially judged to be good would lead to *less* of a desirable outcome. The order of the day was more leads to more, bigger is better, strength leads to strength, and at the same time, less leads to less and weakness leads to weakness.

Because of their devastating destructive power, nuclear weapons altered these long-standing equations governing human warfare. The missiles on one nuclear submarine alone equaled the total destructive power of all the bombs dropped during World War II. Five submarines were sufficient to destroy the two hundred largest Soviet cities. Thus, whether we had fifteen or twenty nuclear subs was not as important as it was in prenuclear days. Even more, if the enemy had ten nuclear subs and we had twenty, it was no longer clear which side was "ahead" or "superior." If the Soviets could hide their subs in the vast oceans of the world, then they would still possess enough power to destroy the United States many times over.

Once the two superpowers reached this level of "awesome destructiveness," then "awesome destructiveness plus one" lost its punch (pun intended). The situation was analogous to the fact that infinity plus one is still infinity.[7]

When More Leads to Less

The situation grew worse as the superpowers realized that "decisive superiority," as measured in traditional terms (such as the total number of nuclear weapons possessed), actually led to greater vulnerability of the recognized superior side. The problem, therefore, could not be posed in traditional terms. It needed to be looked at in a new way, and there were no clear answers.

For example, if only two hundred intercontinental ballistic missiles were sufficient to destroy either side, and the Soviets had ten thousand and the United States had thirty thousand, the Soviets might be tempted to strike first in order to take out all the U.S. missiles, ensuring their survival and superiority. Even though each side could destroy the other hundreds and thousands of times over, the side with the smaller number of nuclear weapons might be tempted to strike first and hence prevail. If a first strike would take out all major cities, what did it matter whether there were enough weapons to retaliate? What would remain that would be worth preserving? But since the same line of reasoning was available to the "superior" side as well, why shouldn't it strike first?

Consider another example: in order to protect their missiles, it made sense for both sides to bury them in the ground in silos. Further, since a silo that had more concrete on top of it was better protected than one with less concrete, it made even more sense to harden silos. More concrete could be seen as better than less because more meant the missiles were better protected. Conversely, less concrete meant less protection. But here again, the logic broke down.

Hardening missile silos produced the opposite of the intended effect. Placing more concrete on top of silos (the right solution to the wrong problem) did not make either side feel more secure in the belief that its silos could take a direct nuclear hit and survive. Placing more concrete on top of silos only led to an increase in the arms race because each side began placing multiple warheads on top of each missile, which meant that each missile packed a greater punch and could penetrate any silo.

The pattern was established: *each move designed to bring more security to one nation led to both sides feeling less secure.* Instead of more leading to more, or greater strength leading to better protection and thereby more security, more led to less. The conventional logic of human warfare that had prevailed for thousands of years was broken. (There are, of course, exceptions to every rule. In *The Art of War*, Sun Tzu showed how fewer soldiers could be an advantage.[8])

Understanding Paradox

In the 1970s I conducted an extensive study of nuclear weapons, and through the course of that study, the issue of arms control became a mirror on the world of paradox.[9] Following are some of the realities that suddenly became clear to me as well as my understanding of how the paradoxes inherent in the development of nuclear weapons and arms control agreements relate to the paradoxes faced by developing organizations in the Systems Age.

Paradox Is Pervasive

For every argument that was made about the properties of nuclear weapons, strategies for their use or nonuse, or the control and prevention of nuclear war, there was an equally compelling counterargument. For instance, for every group of reputable experts who argued that more concrete on top of missile silos was a good thing, there was another group of equally reputable experts who argued the reverse, that is, that less concrete was actually better because it threatened the enemy less. Further, the arguments of each group were internally consistent, plausible, and backed up by whatever data existed. Short of an actual war, the very thing no one wanted, there was no way to prove who was correct. Even a war would not prove anything, since all of the proponents would interpret the situation to their benefit, assuming of course they survived.

The numbers and types of contradictions and paradoxes associated with nuclear weapons and arms control were far greater than anyone had previously realized.[10] Instead of contradiction and paradox being the rare by-products of the arguments surrounding nuclear weapons, it became apparent that they are the very essence of nuclear strategy. What is also becoming apparent is that because of the complexities of the systems in which all organizations now operate, paradox is the very essence of organizational strategy as well.

What is also becoming apparent is that because of the complexities of the systems in which all organizations now operate, paradox is the very essence of organizational strategy as well.

Types of Paradox

The vast majority of arguments made about nuclear weapons and arms control fit into one of the following four types:

1. More leads to more.

2. More leads to less.

3. Less leads to more.

4. Less leads to less.

Types 1 and 4 represent the traditional logic of warfare. Types 2 and 3 represent nontraditional thinking.

Type 2—more leads to less—expresses the fact that all entities obey a law of diminishing returns. Once a certain point is reached (point A in figure 7-1), size is no longer an asset. For example, a larger army may be generally superior to a smaller one, but a larger army has more administrative problems: it is harder to clothe, feed, and transport than a smaller one. Thus, according to the paradox expressed by type 2, at a certain point, possibly unknown and unknowable, size turns back on itself to negate whatever virtues it once possessed.

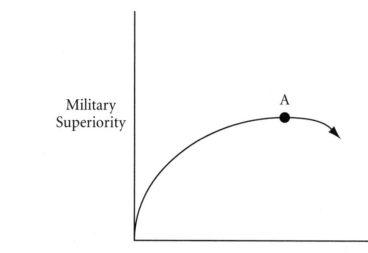

Figure 7-1   *When More Leads to Less*

We encounter this paradox frequently in the world of business. For instance, organizations that grow too fast often experience enormous difficulties in maintaining their core businesses. In short, they outstrip their capabilities to manage larger systems.[11] A recent example is America Online, a subscription service for Internet access, which substantially lowered its monthly service fee in order to sign up new users. So many new customers signed up that the system became overloaded and could not service old or new users properly. Thus, by increasing its subscriber base, America Online created a major crisis for itself, which literally threatened to kill the organization.

This type of paradox is best captured by the notion that "nothing fails so much as overwhelming success." The eminent management consultant Peter Drucker once observed: "Whom the gods want to destroy they send forty years of success." Thus, long periods of unparalleled and unchallenged success (for instance, the forty-year domination of world markets by U.S. car makers) do not make one fit to play in new environments (in Detroit, the challenge to U.S. car makers of small European and Japanese compacts). In more prosaic terms, what has worked well in the past will—I am tempted to say "always will"—lead to failure in the future.[12] Thus, the longer something has worked, the more it deserves to be challenged and regarded with extreme skepticism.

An example of a business whose strategy takes this type of paradox into account is the publisher of this book, Berrett-Koehler, a company that has steadfastly refused to grow larger. Berrett-Koehler sets a strict limit on the number of books it will publish each year. True, it might be able to make more money by publishing more books, but in the process, it might also lose what has made it unique, the ability to deliver special care and quality to each of its authors and hence better serve the reading public.

Type 3—less leads to more—was understood best by the late unorthodox economist E. F. Schumacher. The title of his most famous book, *Small is Beautiful,* captures the idea well.[13] (See curve AB in figure 7-2.) As the second quote at the beginning of this chapter illustrates, Tandy executives didn't appreciate this paradox.

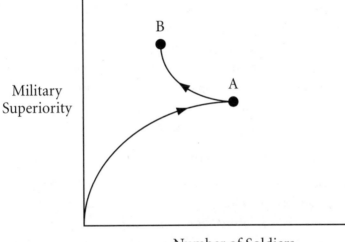

Figure 7-2   *When Less Leads to More*

Iron-Clad Positions Prevent the Acknowledgment of Paradox

In the arms control debate, those who argued that "more leads to more" and "less leads to less" (or "weakness leads to weakness") only rarely admitted the possibilities of "more leads to less" and "less leads to more." These alternate lines of argument, or alternate problem-solving options, were closed off to them. The same was true of those who argued that "more leads to less" and "less leads to more." Each proponent was locked into his or her favorite set of categories, arguments, or options. As a result, each proponent committed an E_3 by not taking into account the positions of their counterparts.

There Is No One "Right" Position

When I looked at the phenomenon of nuclear war and arms control from the standpoint of all four types of paradox, all of the paradoxes were true and false at the same time. Not being locked into one or two of the four types, I was able to see that each captured a partial truth at best. Once again, this meant that unless all four positions were considered simultaneously, E_3 was the inevitable result.

For example, there is a sense in which more concrete on top of silos is better. Once the decision has been made to have missiles, it makes sense to protect them. Thus, more is better (type 1), and less is worse (type 4). However, as a result of improvements in weapons technologies, at some point more becomes less (type 2), and less becomes more (type 3). For instance, less concrete may be less threatening to an opponent, prompting less aggressive behavior, which is actually "more" of a better environment. Since the situation is dynamic and constantly changing, each type of paradox is locked into a vicious dance with each of the others. In fact, we can say that each gives rise to the others because each fuels the dynamics of the situation.

"More" Does Not Diminish Paradox

There seemed to be no hope whatsoever of removing all the contradictions and paradoxes related to nuclear arms and nuclear war. Depending upon an individual's interpretation of the particular phenomenon, "more" to one analyst was often "less" to another analyst, and vice versa. The inherent complexity of the phenomena only intensified long-standing disputes or produced new ones. More contact between analysts and more or better data to review did not by themselves lead to greater clarity and understanding, or fewer paradoxes, and so did not bring clarity to the situation or a greater sense of shared understanding. Unless the proponents could rise above their favorite positions, they were unable to see how they contributed to a collective E_3.

Paradox Must Be Embraced

Traditional thinking, with its natural abhorrence of contradiction and paradox, is not up to the task of dealing with nuclear weapons. For every assertion about nuclear weapons, there is an equally compelling opposite assertion; the situation is entirely unacceptable to traditional logic. If for every argument, A, there is a counterargument, Not-A, it is akin to saying that it is both raining and not raining at the same time in the same place. Conventional logic grinds to a halt.[14] It is as paradoxical as saying that my household pet is both a dog and a chicken (that is, not a dog) at the same time.

The appreciation of paradox was absolutely necessary to break out of a collective E_3. But traditional thinking and paradox are like oil and water: they just don't mix. Since the majority of those who participated in the formulation of nuclear doctrine were educated in traditional thinking, they acknowledged only with great difficulty that nuclear weapons obeyed a different logic. For the most part, they were content to keep contradictions and paradoxes at bay.

Dealing with Paradox Requires a New Perspective

Nuclear weapons existed in order not to be used. Since they couldn't be uninvented Scientifically or Technically, any more than we can uninvent our knowledge of the atom, they had to be reinvented Socially. Because of the growing awareness that they couldn't be used by either side without disastrous consequences to both, no matter who was ahead in the arms race or who started a war first, nuclear weapons began to no longer be regarded as "weapons." Instead, they were reconceptualized as "devices." This reclassification is more than a clever play on words. It expresses a fundamental change in philosophy, which is necessary to avoid committing an E_3. *Reclassifying or relabeling a phenomenon is one of the most important ways of avoiding an E3.*

An understanding of the paradoxes involved in the nuclear arms control issue supplies us with the knowledge necessary to counter two common arguments in our society today: more or bigger is always better, and less is always worse. One example of these arguments is the widely held assumption that there are no problems in U.S. society that cannot be solved through a continually expanding and growing economy. In any complex system, more may lead to more, and less may lead to less. However, we are entitled to conclude that more leads to more and less leads to less only after we have eliminated the possible effects of the other two types of paradoxes.

Placing more concrete on top of silos only led to an increase in the arms race because each side began placing multiple warheads on top of each missile, which meant that each missile packed a greater punch and could penetrate any silo.

The failure to appreciate this fact is responsible for the mismanagement of most complex systems.

Managing Paradox

The following two stories illustrate, respectively, the dangers in today's world of not understanding paradox, and the benefits that can accrue to a business that both understands and manages paradox.

Are More Computers Necessarily Better?

The widespread distribution of computers in classrooms throughout the United States is widely touted as a desirable educational goal. Computer literacy is seen as the solution to many of our problems. Often proponents of this solution fail to take into account the effects on the larger system of the increasing number of computers. The following story, which appeared in the *Los Angeles Times* in October 1996, tells the other side of the story:

Organizations that grow too fast often experience enormous difficulties in maintaining their core business.

> The unrelenting growth of the Internet computer network is severely straining the nation's telecommunication system, causing local phone service failures in some areas and perpetual "brownouts" on the computer network.
>
> The congestion is especially acute in California, which has a higher proportion of Internet users than any other region of the country. A recent study by Pacific Telesis in the Silicon Valley found that 1/6 of local telephone calls did not connect, yielding either a "fast busy" signal or nothing at all. . . .
>
> "We're coming close to gridlock," says Amir Atai, Director of Network and Traffic Performance at Bellcore. "It won't make a difference to the person who is already on line, but what about the next user who is trying to make a 911 call?"[15]

The Right Way to Grow

A recent feature story in *Fortune* magazine about Starbucks coffee chain not only reinforces the general points of this chapter but also shows that, if done right, bigger can sometimes be better. Growth must be managed carefully, however, and this is done by gaining an understanding of the *detailed processes* within which growth can be managed.

Starbucks, the 25-year-old coffee bar chain with the high-caffeine growth rate, has expanded at an annual pace of over

50% since 1987, mainly through perfecting new ways of delivering one of the oldest commodities known to man.

[Companies that grow] share several fundamental traits. *They have stable, experienced management teams, they spend heavily on R&D, and they invest a great deal of energy and money in recruiting and training employees. Above all, they realize that growth doesn't just happen. It has to be planned, nurtured, measured, and rewarded.* . . . [Emphasis added.]

Starbucks keeps its channel flowing smoothly by deliberately restricting its growth. Yes, it's hard to believe a company that is expanding 50% per year is limiting anything, but Starbucks won't franchise, won't artificially flavor its coffees, won't join hands with most of the hundreds of would-be partners who bang on its doors each week—stores, restaurants, airlines, hotels, and gas stations—all anxious to piggyback on Starbucks' good name. Explains the CEO, "Over the short term these steps would drive up revenues and profits. But over the long term they would be a giant mistake." [Starbucks' CEO] fears that if he grows too fast, he'll lose control over quality and tarnish his company's upscale image. That's why you won't see Starbucks coffee being sold in a 7-Eleven.[16]

In a word, an organization can grow, bigger can be better, but if and only if the organization understands, and hence manages carefully, the underlying processes (culture, infrastructure, innovation) that lead to profitable growth. Growth for its own sake, and without proper management controls, more often than not leads to less. (See the story of America Online on page 106.)

Conclusion

Russell Ackoff has identified four stages through which all organizations pass: (1) survival, (2) viability, (3) growth, and (4) development. In the *survival* stage, a fledgling organization has to be supported by external sources because it is not yet strong enough to exist on its own, that is, its losses exceed its revenues. In *viability,* an organization is just starting to take off; it is only just "in the black." During *growth,* an organization is clearly in the stage where more or bigger leads to more. *Development,* on the other hand, means an organization has to learn to do more with less. It has reached the point where it can no longer continue to grow, at least not substantially with its traditional products, services, and organizational structure.

Russell Ackoff argues persuasively that all organizations are always steering a course between these four stages.[17] When an organization has finally become viable, there is, of course, the danger that it will slip back into the survival stage. When an organization is in the growth cycle, it can anticipate decline and thereby move to the development stage.

An appreciation of the paradox in the relationship of these four stages is absolutely essential to managing an organization in the Systems Age, the age of complexity. As Ackoff puts it, "Cemeteries and garbage heaps grow each year, but they don't develop." The moral: if you want to keep on growing, and especially if you want to grow fast, slow down!

An appreciation of paradox is also essential to the recognition of false paradoxes or absurdities. Recall from the Vietnam war that the destruction of the tiny village of My Lai was justified with the bizarre reasoning "The village had to be destroyed in order to save it." I believe that this same reasoning, which I call the My Lai Theory of Organizations, lies unrecognized beneath many of the current strategies to salvage organizations, and downsizing is a perfect example: an organization has to be downsized—read destroyed—in order to save it!

Critical Questions for You and Your Organization

1. Make a list of the major paradoxes that confront you and your organization.

2. List some examples of situations where you and your organization got caught up in "bigger or more is better." Why?

3. List some of the ways in which bigger or more has led to less. Why?

4. List some of the ways in which you and your organization could benefit from "less is more." Why?

Systems Thinking for the Systems Age

PART THREE

Part three discusses methods that individuals and organizations can use to think systemically—to see how the parts fit into the whole—and shows how systems thinking is the best, if not the only, way to formulate problems correctly in today's Systems Age.

Chapter 8 discusses two different methods that organizations can use to manage problems, both of which encourage looking at situations from multiple perspectives, and both of which reduce the chances of solving the wrong problem precisely.

Chapter 9 discusses some of the reasons why we are addicted to outmoded Machine Age thinking, what Systems Age thinking actually is, and how we can break through to thinking systemically.

CHAPTER 8

Managing Problems from Multiple Perspectives

Dutch academic Geert Hofstede, who studied European cultural differences for U.S. computer giant International Business Machines Corp. in the 1970s and later emerged as one of the leading experts in the field, has argued that Europeans remain inevitably divided by their history.

Countries have remained separate precisely because there existed fundamental differences in thinking and feeling between them. . . .

—Tyler Marshall,
Los Angeles Times

It must be considered that there is nothing more difficult to carry out, nor more doubtful of success, nor more dangerous to handle, than to initiate a new order of things. For the reformer has enemies in all those who profit by the old order, and only lukewarm defenders in all those who would profit by the new order, this lukewarmness arising partly from fear of their adversaries, who have the laws in their favor; and partly from the incredulity of mankind, who do not truly believe in anything new until they have had actual experience of it.

—Niccolo Machiavelli,
The Prince

THERE ARE NO MAGIC BROMIDES that will guarantee we will avoid all E_3s. To be human is to commit errors. Wisdom is the ability to learn from those errors; spirituality, the ability to forgive them in oneself and in others.[1]

Although there are no guaranteed ways to avoid E_3s, there are ways to challenge a person's, a group's, an institution's, or a society's view of its problems. As time goes on, those ways of challenging can themselves be challenged ad infinitum. This is because the methods for challenging our ideas are not perfect and hence are themselves in need of constant challenge and continual development.

We do not require perfection in order to manage E_3. We merely require methods that can challenge our ideas as best as is humanly possible at the present time.

Over the years, my colleagues and I have investigated a number of methods for producing dramatically different views of important problems.[2] In this book, I want to present two of those methods. The first derives from an interpretation and extension of Jungian psychology that delineates personality types;[3] the second is a special interpretation of strategic management.

Jung's Personality Types

An individual's personality affects his or her behavior, and as a result personality affects how an individual sees problems and goes about solving them. If an organization consists mainly of people with a single personality type, problems will be seen in only one way, thus providing fertile ground for solving the wrong problems. This risk is mitigated by having a diverse group of personality types who can challenge one another's perspectives.

Insight into diverse personality types is provided by the work of Carl Jung, the Swiss psychiatrist who was initially a close friend and working colleague of Sigmund Freud. At one point in time, Jung was selected by Freud to be his official successor. Later, when the two men differed strongly in their interpretations of psychoanalysis, they unfortunately became bitter enemies.

In addition to his pioneering work in psychoanalysis, Jung also developed a fascinating framework, or system, for capturing the enduring differences between people.[4] It is an obvious fact of human existence that people differ in their basic makeup. It was Jung's genius to see how differences

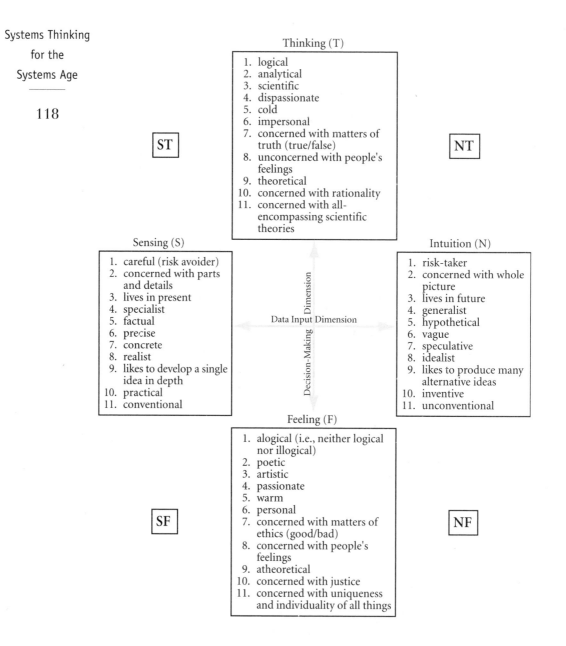

Figure 8-1   The Jungian Dimensions

in temperament, which manifest themselves in every field of human endeavor, could be captured in four salient dimensions, two of which are shown in figure 8-1.[5]

Each of the dimensions contributes something to an individual's decision-making process. The first dimension, data input (the horizontal dimension in figure 8-1), describes not only the kinds of data some people initially take in but, more fundamentally, what they regard as data in the first place. Once a person has taken in data, the second dimension, decision making (the vertical dimension in figure 8-1), refers to how a person processes the data. The third dimension, which is not shown in figure 8-1, is orientation to self and the world, which is either from the inside out or from the outside in. The fourth dimension, which is also not shown, is strength. This dimension describes whether a person's preference for gathering data is stronger or weaker than his or her preference for making decisions.

Data Input: Sensing versus Intuition

The data input dimension refers to two distinct and opposite ways of gathering information—sensing and intuition. People who are characterized as Sensing (S) types take a complex situation, or a whole system, and break it down into its constituent parts or components. The parts are then assessed in terms of numbers and facts. The numbers and facts are *information* for those with a strong Sensing orientation.

Intuitive (N) types are the opposite of S types. Whereas S types break complex situations or systems down into their component parts, N types synthesize details into wholes or larger patterns. Whereas only concrete particulars are real to an S, only larger wholes are real to an N. Whereas only that which already exists in the here-and-now and can be measured in terms of the human senses is real to an S, imagined future, hypothetical possibilities are real to an N. In other words, possibilities themselves are information to Ns. For example, currently well-understood technologies, such as the conventional gasoline engine, are real to an S, while future modes of transportation, such as hybrid electric-gasoline cars, are real to an N.

As Jung constantly emphasized, one type is not right and the other wrong in how they view and experience the world; they are merely different. Either perspective can be right or wrong depending on the situation. We can say that by virtue of their complexity, all situations can be analyzed from both an S and an N perspective.

Decision Making: Thinking versus Feeling

The decision-making dimension (see figure 8-1) is bounded by two distinct ways of reaching decisions: Thinking (T) and Feeling (F). However we take in information, and whatever we call information, there are two opposite ways of reaching a decision with regard to that information. If we analyze data according to impersonal formulas, rules, or abstract logic that supposedly applies to all people and to problems in all situations, then we are a Thinking type. If, on the other hand, we make decisions based on personal considerations and feelings, personal likes and dislikes, we are a Feeling type.

Once again, one approach isn't better than the other; they are merely different. Given the complexity of the world, all decisions can be examined from both a T and an F perspective.

Since all situations have both T and F aspects, one can pick any situation to illustrate how T and F personality types see the world differently. A personal favorite of mine is the following story about a couple who attended a dinner party with my wife, Donna, and me:

> After dinner, we witnessed an unfortunate replay of an argument between the couple. A few nights before, the wife had gone out for the evening and left her husband to care for their two small children. She returned home much earlier than she had planned and was horrified to find that her two small children had been left alone. The husband had ducked out for a few minutes to go to his office to pick up some important papers on which he was working. When he returned home, his wife was furious. The husband's rationale was this: "I figured that the probability of anything happening to the children was only one in ten thousand."

In the years since this incident happened, I have used it repeatedly in classes and workshops to illustrate the differences, to put it mildly, between T and F types. The wife was horrified at her husband's T logic. What made the situation even worse, and hence more tense, was the fact that the wife felt at a loss to counter her husband, who was a scientist. She knew instinctively that he was wrong, but she lacked both the basic vocabulary and the self-esteem to say how or why. As a result, she was unable to utter the following, which is my retort, although her every word and manner implied it:

> Let me tell you why I am so outraged. First of all, I don't have ten thousand children. Even if I did, I wouldn't want to sacrifice any of them, as the main female character in the movie *Sophie's Choice* had to do. Second, you're looking at the denom-

inator in this situation, the ten thousand. I'm looking at the numerator. I have only one pair of children who are precious to me. They are absolutely unique. They are the only "ones" of their kind. Putting the situation in the way you did utterly trivializes their humanity. You have reduced a human situation to a game of chance. That is absolutely intolerable!

The moral of this story is not that F types are always right and T types are always wrong. *In this particular case,* T was wrong, especially since he couldn't see the Feeling components of the situation. I could give just as many examples where F is wrong as where T is wrong. If I am overly critical of T types, it is only because they are so dominant in our culture. Being a Thinking type myself, and having been surrounded by them throughout my educational and professional life, I'm entitled to be critical.

Introvert versus Extrovert

The dimension of orientation to self and the world is also bounded by two distinct and opposite types: Introvert (I) and Extrovert (E). Contrary to popular misconception, Introverts are not generally shy and withdrawn, and Extroverts are not generally outgoing and gregarious. This is not what Jung meant by I and E.

Wisdom is the ability to learn from errors; spirituality, the ability to forgive them in oneself and in others.

According to Jung, Introverts are their own ultimate judges as to the reality, importance, or correctness of a situation. Whether others agree with them or not is entirely beside the point because Introverts go with their own assessments and judgments. Extroverts, on the other hand, are especially tuned in and extremely sensitive to what others think or feel. They rely on and mirror the thoughts, feelings, and opinions of the larger society. For instance, if an Introvert feels that pornography is wrong, then it doesn't matter what others think or believe. For Extroverts, contemporary community standards are all important. If the community feels that pornography is okay, then it is all right with them.

Perception versus Judgment

The strength dimension, which does not come from Jung but from those who extended his ideas, refers to the fact that for some people the data input dimension is stronger than the decision-making dimension, while for others the reverse is true.[6] If the data input dimension is stronger, that is called Perception (P), and if the decision-making dimension is stronger, that is called Judging (J). P types like to go on collecting data forever without ever making a decision. (For this reason, one of my students called P the Procrastination dimension.) J types feel comfortable in making decisions based on little or no data.

An SP type (Sensing, Perception) always has one more fact to collect before feeling comfortable in making a decision. On the other hand, an NP type (Intuitive, Perception) always has one more future possibility to be imagined before making a decision. Meanwhile, TJs (Thinking, Judging) easily make decisions based on T considerations alone, while FJs (Feeling, Judging) make decisions on F considerations alone.

The Four Basic Personality Types

Putting the various combinations together results in sixteen different personality types. This means that both in theory and in actuality, there are at least sixteen different ways of looking at and analyzing any situation! At one time or another, my colleagues and I have used all sixteen types to analyze complex problems and hence to minimize E_3. As a practical matter, however, sixteen views are too many to handle; four are more manageable. For this reason, we have chosen four perspectives that we generally use: ST, NT, NF, and SF.

In our teaching and consulting work, in order to demonstrate how differently these personality types approach problem solving, we begin with a short test that assesses a person's Jungian type. We then put all those of a similar type into a common group. That is, all the STs are put in one group, all the NTs in another, and so on. We then ask each group to analyze a complex situation, define what they perceive the problems to be, and suggest possible solutions based on their perspectives. If the groups are open and venturesome, we even give each of them a Tinkertoy set and ask them to build something that best represents their view of the problem and to list as many characteristics of both the problem and the solution as possible.

Only after each group has presented its views do we explain the Jungian system and how the groups were put together. We explain that putting like types together in a common group accentuates what they have in common—they all speak the same psychological language and hence tend to see the world similarly—and it accentuates the differences between the various types. Also, asking people to build something and to list characteristics allows people to see what is one of the most difficult of all things to observe: human personality.

The fact that there are no experts in Tinkertoys, and that there is no right or wrong way to build a perception of a problem with Tinkertoys, allows each group to project its type onto a common and neutral screen. Because the Tinkertoy constructions, the descriptions, and the definitions of the problems are generally so different, we ask the participants to describe in their words what they have seen and heard after all of the groups have given short presentations. As a general rule, people are absolutely mystified that different groups see the world so differently. They discover that even though they are all speaking English, the words don't have the same meanings. Contrary to popular opinion, the most difficult translations occur between those who think they are speaking the same language when in fact they are not.

Mystification turns to outright shock when a cover is removed from a flip chart containing previously written predictions regarding what each of the four types would select as a problem, its list of detailed characteristics of the problems, and the general nature and shape of its construction.

SENSING, THINKING TYPES (STs)

STs generally focus on technical problems (for example, economic or scientific), which can be defined precisely in terms of conventional knowledge and technology. Above all, they are reductionists. They break all problems down into separable and manageable components. They believe that a system is never more than the sum of its independent parts.

The constructions of STs are generally symmetrical, reflecting their strong preference for order and control. This need is so great that often, without instruction, the very first thing they do is dump all of the Tinkertoy parts out of the container in which they came and line them up in neat and tidy groups! They take a precise inventory of all the parts and agree without much discussion among the group members that their construction shall use no more and no less than the parts they have been given.

INTUITIVE, THINKING TYPES (NTs)

NTs also define their problems in technical terms. Whereas STs define their problems in terms of today's knowledge and break things down into small, independent parts, however, NTs define their problems in terms of the far-out technology of the future and take broad systems as a whole into consideration. Their constructions are not as symmetrical, indicating that they think "outside of the box." They also incorporate objects that they happen to have with them, such as pictures, pens, and so on, into their constructions.

INTUITIVE, FEELING TYPES (NFs)

NFs also think in terms of large, whole systems. But instead of technology, they focus on people and the largest human group possible, humanity. They are concerned with broad issues affecting equity, fairness, and justice. Their constructions are generally the most asymmetrical of all the groups, reflecting their almost complete disdain for traditional structures that cramp and inhibit feeling.

SENSING, FEELING TYPES (SFs)

SFs, like STs, are concerned with details and parts, except that their units of analysis are human, not technical. Whereas NFs are concerned with all of humanity, SFs don't believe in such abstractions. They believe that only individuals and families matter. Everything must be traced back to these units, which alone have existence for them. Their constructions also tend to be symmetrical, reflecting the love and trust between specific, individual persons about whom they care deeply. In contrast, NFs preach harmony, love, and trust for all of humankind.

An individual's personality affects his or her behavior, and as a result personality affects how an individual sees problems and goes about solving them.

Diversity in an Organization and E₃

If an organization has enough diversity in its members, then it can generally produce four very different definitions of its problems, reflecting the four basic personality types. If for political and cultural reasons, however, it cannot assemble two or more different personality types, then an E_3 will more likely occur, with possible implications for the broader society. For example, a former student of mine, Charles Matthews, did a small study of savings and loans (S&Ls). Discounting outright thievery, he found that those S&Ls that failed had a narrow collection of Jungian types among their top executives, while those that survived and prospered had a broad collection of types, which permitted the executives to challenge their basic business strategies because they challenged the basic definitions of their business problems. Problems truly are inside of us.

If an organization cannot form two or more different groups from among its current personnel to examine its problems from different perspectives, then this inability is one of its most basic problems! Its major E_3 is thinking it can solve all its other problems without first solving the problem of how to get a broader range of personality types into its organization.

Strategic Management

Analysis based on strategic management is another method of challenging a person's or an institution's way of viewing its problems. Strategic management is concerned with formulating and examining a set of diverse policy options to guide the organization's future.

Using this basic concept, any complex issue or problem can be approached from four different policy perspectives:

- The Status Quo
- Moderate Change
- Substantial Change
- Complete or Radical Change

There are several reasons for examining problems from these four perspectives. As one of the introductory quotes to this chapter illustrates, Machiavelli understood well that change is one of the most difficult issues facing all individuals and organizations. Changing policy often means changing an individual's lifestyle and an organization's structure and is never to be taken lightly or assumed. The status quo, as a "known evil," already has a set of defenders and an infrastructure, the organization, which has been designed to promote it actively. The status quo thus has a strong appeal and is often preferable to the unknown. Even if the status quo is unsatisfactory, it still deserves its day in court; an explicit defense of the status quo can systematically expose its strengths and its weaknesses.

By the same token, different degrees of change need to be considered precisely because change arouses high anxieties, fears, and resistance. As a result, change is often not considered at all or is given shoddy or superficial consideration so that it can be rejected easily.

When examining situations or problems with this method, individuals can be assigned to four different groups based on the four different policy perspectives listed above. Each group is then instructed to analyze and make the strongest case for formulating and addressing an organization's problems in terms of the particular policy perspective to which it has been assigned.

In examining problems from these four perspectives, it is possible to assign individuals to a group based on their Jungian type. For instance, an S (Sensing) typically prefers the currently known world, or the status quo, to the unknown, and an N (Intuitive) prefers the future to the present, favoring complete or radical change. Individuals can also be assigned randomly in order to force everyone, no matter what his or her personality, to confront different degrees of change. In arguing for problem formulation and solution from a particular policy perspective, it is not necessary to believe in that perspective, only to make the argument for it. The rationale for this is that those who oppose a position can often make the strongest case for it.

In *The Unbounded Mind,* I described an additional process through which I have taken strategic management or policy groups.[7] Each of the four policy groups is asked to list as many stakeholders as it can upon whom its policy option depends for support or whose opposition it must overcome. Next, the groups are asked to state what they either know or must assume about each stakeholder in order to make the strongest case for their policy option. Finally, they are asked to plot their assumptions on a special chart so that the entire belief system that underlies their option can be seen. In effect, the chart is a way of bringing hidden assumptions to the surface so that they can be visualized, much as Tinkertoys help us to see personality differences.

After the four belief systems that underlie the policy options are seen, an extensive debate is conducted over the differences in assumptions that divide the groups. Then the groups are recomposed and a new competition takes place. Given the debate that the group as a whole has witnessed, the question becomes, What is the best new, combined option we would recommend for our organization and why? In other words, given the explicit knowledge of these four different ways of viewing the world, can the four views be integrated into a new view that goes beyond any one of them? Or, what is the best that can be done at the present time? The following example illustrates a positive application of this approach.

Managing the Design of the U.S. Census

Vincent Barabba is currently the general manager of Strategy and Knowledge Development for General Motors. As such, he arguably holds the most important market intelligence job in the United States, if not the world.

Before coming to GM, Vince held similar posts at Eastman Kodak and Xerox. Before that, he was director of the U.S. Bureau of the Census in both the Nixon and the Carter administrations, where he was responsible for conducting the census in 1980 and in 1990, both of which were billion-dollar operations.

Although a Republican, Vince was brought into the Carter adminis-tration because of his extraordinary skills in diffusing political criticism. In recent years, the taking of a census has become a political minefield because of the difficulties in counting everyone in a society as diverse and complex as ours.[8] Literally hundreds of billions of dollars in block grants, as well as congressional apportionments, depend upon an accurate count of citizens. Little wonder, then, why in recent years the mayors of large cities have sued the Bureau of the Census, alleging that it has missed or undercounted important groups, most notably blacks and Hispanics.

During his two terms at the Bureau of the Census, Vince was respon-sible for overseeing the design and conducting the census in both 1980 and 1990. One major problem with conducting a national census is deceptively easy to state but hellishly difficult to resolve. From separate cross-checking surveys that the bureau regularly conducts, the bureau believes that approximately 2 percent of the white population and approximately 8 per-cent of the black and Hispanic populations are undercounted when the national census is conducted every ten years. Why then not correct the raw census counts by multiplying by 1.02 for whites and by 1.08 for blacks and Hispanics? As with most simple solutions, this tactic actually makes the problem worse. The percents of undercounts are *estimates* of the *national undercounts* of whites, blacks, and Hispanics. In some localities, whites are missed by more than 2 percent and in other localities by less than 2 per-cent. The same is true for blacks and Hispanics. Multiplying indiscrimi-nately by constant factors would make some localities worse off and some better off than they actually are.

The problem quickly becomes even juicier. The Census Bureau has devised four broad strategies for responding to the undercount. All are controversial.

The first strategy is to go with the raw census counts even though it is known that they miss counting persons who should be counted. The raw counts at least count real persons and not hypothetical missed persons. In other words, go with what a census enumerator has actually observed or has heard in direct testimony as to the existence of other family members or relatives.

The remaining three strategies consist of various theoretical options for estimating the numbers of persons who are missed by direct enumera-tion. The three strategies differ with regard to how extreme or radical they are in correcting for uncounted persons. In effect, the strategies range from the most conservative methods for attributing persons to the most radical, that is, at the cutting edge of statistical methodology.

Because the stakes are so high, statisticians have begrudgingly come to realize that the taking of a census is not a purely scientific or technical problem; it is a complex mixture of economic, legal, political, scientific, social, and technical issues.

To decide which method the Census Bureau would use in reporting the census, Barabba, Richard O. Mason, and I conducted a special planning conference.[9] Fifty people attended a week-long exercise where each of the four alternatives was examined and then hotly debated. Thirty-five of the attendees were from the top executive staff of the Census Bureau. Fifteen were outside users of Census Bureau data who, at the time, were all engaged in suing the bureau over its alleged failure to count persons in their locales or to adjust the actual counts to their satisfaction. The decision was made to include the fifteen in the formulation of the Census Bureau's strategies precisely because their viewpoints were different!

The data input dimension refers to two distinct and opposite ways of gathering information—sensation and intuition.

Each of the fifty individuals was assigned at random to one of the four strategy options. All were asked to make the strongest case for the option to which they were assigned. It was not necessary for them to believe in the absolute truth of their option, only to argue persuasively for it. In addition, the fifteen outsiders were told that the bureau did not expect them to end their lawsuits at the end of the conference. They were invited to participate because they had expert knowledge or a critical perspective on the issue that the bureau did not. They were actually encouraged to go ahead with their suits since they had the power to force changes in the bureau's operation that it could not achieve on its own but desired nonetheless. In other words, the fifteen were highly relevant precisely because their interests were not the same!

As a result of the conference, the bureau finally made the decision to go with the raw census counts as the best available option. The decision was published, along with its underlying rationale, in *The Federal Register.* Those who disagreed with this decision could certainly do so, but they had to make a case against the underlying rationale. In this way, while further controversy was not avoided altogether, it was at least made more manageable.

Strategic Management at General Motors

Drawing upon his experience at the Census Bureau and in other organizations, Vince has founded the GM Knowledge Network.[10] In many ways, it is a strategic organizational site for problem finding and problem formulation. One of its primary purposes is to bring order to the disparate and vast array of marketing studies that GM has conducted over the years. Before Vince, these studies were never viewed as an integrated whole, and thus were never able to give GM the kind of accurate customer information needed to build cars that people would buy. *What good does it do to build the best cars that no one wants? Building such cars is the solution to the wrong problem.*

Vince has not only brought order to GM's current marketing surveys, but he has gone back into GM's vast archives to discover missed opportunities and to probe why they were never exploited. For instance, in 1938, customers were asked on surveys to sketch cars they would be interested in owning. One sketch is unmistakable: it is a rendition of what would later become the popular VW van. Why did GM, as many large organizations do, ignore such ideas?

In sum, at GM, Vince did not fall into the trap of solving the wrong marketing problems one at a time and independently of one another. He not only looked at GM's marketing problems as a whole, but he explicitly set up a new and innovative problem-solving center for the express purpose of minimizing E_3.

Lesson Number Seven: If at all possible, include those who are in active opposition to one's policies in a strategic planning initiative; if their direct participation is not possible, then have someone role-play their reasonable participation, that is, what is reasonable from their point of view.

A Jungian Analysis of Downsizing

To show further how the ideas in this chapter can be applied, let us briefly consider the issue of downsizing from the point of view of the Jungian types.

STs (Sensing, Thinking) view downsizing as an effective means of cutting costs. True to form, they typically define downsizing strictly, and solely, in financial terms. As a result, they tend to ignore the human or social costs of both their definition of and their solution to the problem. Furthermore, because it is both simple and clear-cut, once they have locked onto downsizing as a strategy, they rarely consider other alternatives.

NTs (Intuitive, Thinking) typically ask whether new businesses can be invented that will make downsizing unnecessary. They also consider the impacts of downsizing on the organization as a total system. They are generally reluctant to employ downsizing unless it can be shown that no other alternatives are available, for instance, that no new businesses can be invented or no alternate variables are responsible for the unprofitability of an organization.

NFs (Intuitive, Feeling) are especially concerned about the effects of downsizing on the larger community in which the organization resides, whether downsizing will cause more social problems and, hence, actually increase costs. NFs are especially interested in whether an organization's culture is primarily responsible for its poor financial performance. NFs typically insist that everyone take a pay cut before anyone is fired. This follows from their basic concern with equity, fairness, and justice. Finally, they are concerned with the effects of downsizing on organizational trust.

SFs (Sensing, Feeling) stress the grieving and healing that will have to take place as a result of downsizing. To them, downsizing is akin to murdering the members of their family. Like NFs, they support pay cuts instead of killing the spirit of an organization.

Thus, if an organization consists primarily of one personality type, its choice of a solution may be almost involuntary; it goes unchallenged and thus an E_3 occurs.

Jungian Analysis of Problems and Solutions

The Jungian framework helps to shed light on two important questions: (1) What is a problem? and (2) What is a solution? As we shall see, each of the four personality types can be lined up with one of the four problem-solving perspectives outlined in Figure 4-3, Scientific/Technical, Interpersonal/Social, Existential, and Systemic. Why people choose certain perspectives can be explained using Jungian analysis. In addition, each of the personality types tends to define the notion of a solution differently, which is reflected in the English language through the use of several variations of the verb *to solve*—absolve, dissolve, and resolve. Both a person's problem-solving perspective and one's view of what constitutes a solution affect how one goes about formulating and solving problems, which in turn affects the likelihood of committing an E_3.

Ralph Kilmann notes that there is a close, if not intimate, connection between *problems* and *opportunities*. Both problems and opportunities exist when there is a gap between our ideals (what we would like to achieve) and what is. A problem exists when we are dissatisfied with our current state. An opportunity exists when our current state is satisfactory, but we would like to make it better.

I use the term *problem* to refer to both problems and opportunities because E_3 applies equally to both.

Jungian Analysis and Solutions

To solve a problem means to bring our current state up to the level of our ideal state so that there is no longer a significant gap between our ideals and our reality. This is often impossible to do because to achieve an exact solution to a problem may impose too severe a constraint. For this reason, the English language contains some important nuances with respect to the verb *to solve:* absolve, dissolve, and resolve.

To absolve means to forgive or to stop blaming a stakeholder or a set of stakeholders associated with a particular problem.

To resolve a problem does not mean to eliminate it altogether, but rather to contain it within generally accepted limits. Thus, modern democratic economies tolerate an unemployment rate within acceptable limits, for example, lower than 2 to 4 percent. To get the unemployment rate to drop significantly below this range is seen not only to be too difficult but also to lead to even worse problems.

To dissolve a problem means something much different. A problem may be dissolved if it becomes less important than it once was. Thus, a problem may remain as large as it was initially and not able to be contained within acceptable limits, but viewed against the broader fabric or system of other problems, it may no longer be important enough either to solve or to resolve. A controversial example is the legalization of alcohol and even of drugs. The levels of alcoholism or drug abuse may remain the same as before, but once sale and distribution are legalized, the drinking of alcohol or the use of drugs is no longer viewed as a punishable crime.

These variations on possible solutions are important to recognize because it may be that many, if not most, important problems are not solvable in the strict sense of the word. Instead of their complete elimination or absolute containment, we constantly have to manage critical problems as best we can given our resources and capabilities. For example, we may never be able to solve the abortion or the teenage pregnancy problems to the satisfaction of all stakeholders. Some people's insistence that we do is itself a big part of the problem. How to get a general populace to recognize the different senses of the verb *to solve,* and to recognize which ones apply in which situations, is another important problem—one that itself has to be continually formulated and managed.

How does Jung fit into all of this? It should be apparent by now that each of the various Jungian personality types insists on a different sense of the verb *to solve.* STs (Sensing, Thinking) generally insist on the strict sense of solution before they consider a problem truly solved. NTs (Intuitive, Thinking) favor dissolution and resolution. NFs (Intuitive, Feeling) favor absolution, dissolution, and resolution. And finally, SFs (Sensing, Feeling) favor absolution, dissolution, and resolution.

Jungian Analysis and Problem Definition

As I said before, figure 4-3 in chapter 4 shows the four problem-solving perspectives: Scientific/Technical, Interpersonal/Social, Existential, and Systemic. These four perspectives generally (although not completely) line up with the Jungian dimensions in Figure 8-1. As shown in Figure 8-2, the Scientific/Technical–Interpersonal/Social perspective is the least controversial. It easily corresponds with the Jungian dimensions of Thinking (T) and Feeling (F). The Existential–Systemic perspective is a bit more complicated. Existential can be identified with Sensing (S) to a degree because answers to life's basic existential questions give one a basic sense of not only purpose but *grounding.* It is in this sense that existential is taken

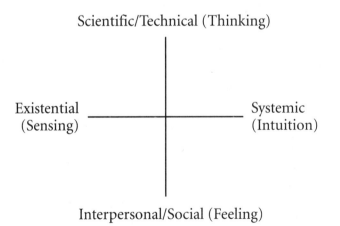

Figure 8-2   A Jungian Analysis of the Four Perspectives on Any Problem

to line up with S. In the same sense, Systemic can line up with Intuitive (N) because it deals with the broader context in which everything exists.

It needs to be emphasized, however, that unlike the four Jungian dimensions, the four perspectives on problems in figure 8-2 are not completely independent. For example, it is possible to give Scientific/Technical explanations of Interpersonal/Social issues. Indeed, this is what a great deal of social science research is about. The two ends of the perspective are distinct in the sense that having Scientific/Technical knowledge does not automatically make one better at Interpersonal/Social relations, although it can help.

More importantly, the four ends of the dimensions in figure 8-2 can be combined, in a similar manner to the four ends in figure 8-1, in endless ways to elucidate problems. Thus, for instance, the Interpersonal/Social perspective includes not only personal issues but also larger ethical and moral issues (Feeling). Whereas Scientific/Technical inquiries can be used to develop formal theories of ethics, the opposite pole, Interpersonal/Social, concerns one's own personal morality.

The Existential and Interpersonal/Social perspectives can be combined to elucidate one of the most difficult of all areas, aesthetics. Here we are dealing with questions of mood as much as the formal issues of aesthetics, for example, what is generally pleasing to oneself and to others.

The point of figure 8-2 is that the four ends of the dimensions identify four generic and very different perspectives on problems, as well as at least four different types of E_3. For example, one of the major forms of E_3 is saying a problem is Scientific/Technical when it is actually Interpersonal/Social. The same is true for the other combinations. By showing the four perspectives with the four Jungian types, we can see more clearly how a particular personality type affects a person's perspective on a problem, and we can see the kind of E_3 that type is most likely to commit.

It is not possible to overemphasize the importance of psychology in the perception of problems and their solutions. Many scientists and technicians confuse their own perceptions with those of the public. As a result, they are often shocked to find that unless they have made contact with public emotion (Feeling) on an issue, the public not only will be turned off to valid scientific data but will be extremely hostile to it and to the scientists who produced it. All the valid scientific data and reasoning in the world (Sensing, Thinking) is irrelevant if it is not conveyed in a style that will allow people to receive it (Feeling).

If we analyze data according to impersonal formulas, rules, or abstract logic that supposedly applies to all people and to problems in all situations, then we are a Thinking type. If, on the other hand, we make decisions based on personal considerations and feelings, personal likes and dislikes, we are a Feeling type.

The most controversial implication here is that ST (Sensing, Thinking) is the epitome of Machine Age thinking, while NT (Intuitive, Thinking) and NF (Intuitive, Feeling) are the epitome of Systems Age thinking. If this is true, STs cannot be put in charge of managing problem-solving processes. Since they typically believe that there is one and only one formulation and solution to every important problem, they inherently limit the exploration of important problems. This does not mean that STs do not have an important role to play in the problem-solving process, only that they cannot lead it.

Conclusion

Conflicts arise daily within and between individuals, groups, and societies. Unfortunately, most conflicts are unproductive, but they need not be. When humans have access to processes whereby they can develop differences systematically and then display them, it is possible to argue fruitfully, that is, to engage in productive conflict. Only after different views have been produced systematically can we explore new definitions. In other words, the purpose of producing differences is not for the sake of producing differences. The purpose is to see if we can open up new possibilities for solutions to problems that integrate basic differences in perception.

Can we ever be completely sure that we have produced *at least two* different formulations of a problem? If we want to be "completely sure," then the answer is, "Of course not!" But we can know that if we use a different formulation, then we get a different solution. Thus, a formulation of a problem that angers, annoys, or disturbs us is an indication that it is different from our normal perception. The fact that we have no way of guaranteeing absolutely that we can always produce two different alternatives in all cases does not mean that we are powerless to discern differences. In every case, we do the best that we can.

Critical Questions for You and Your Organization

1. Pick an important problem with which you and your organization have been struggling. Define it from the vantage point of the four Jungian personality types that were discussed in this chapter.

2. For this same problem, produce an integrated definition of the problem.

3. What do these different definitions tell you about the problem and the ways in which you and your organization have attempted to solve the problem in the past?

4. Which types of definitions do you and your organization typically prefer? Why?

5. What can you do to ensure that other ways of defining important problems are acknowledged by your organization?

CHAPTER 9

Developing New Ways of Thinking Systemically

"Oh God, how grandiose, to be the keeper of the American value system," said Steve Race, President of Sony Computer Entertainment. "I just sell [video] games, lady. To make me responsible for the mores or values of America, I don't think I'm ready for that."

> —Amy Harmon,
> *Los Angeles Times*

It is possible to be a master in false philosophy—easier, in fact, than to be a master in the truth—because a false philosophy can be made as simple and consistent as one pleases.

> —George Santayana,
> *Character and Opinion in the United States*

AS WE HAVE EMPHASIZED REPEATEDLY, in today's Systems Age everything is interconnected. Why then do so many individuals persist in holding on to Machine Age thinking? Why are our taken-for-granted assumptions not challenged rigorously? Why is ethics not included automatically as part of the formulation of important problems? The answers to these questions lie in the outmoded thought processes we use to solve problems and in the dysfunctional behavior of many organizations. These topics and how we can break through to thinking systemically are the subjects of this chapter.

Five Ways of Thinking

In *The Unbounded Mind,* Hal Linstone and I describe the following five archetypal ways of thinking or reaching decisions, which derive from the history of Western philosophy:[1]

- Expert Consensus
- Expert Modeling
- Multiple Models
- Conflict
- Systemic Reasoning

These different ways of thinking are so basic that they pervade all of the decision-making and problem-solving methods of the Western world, but E_3 can only be assessed through the use of certain of these ways. Worst of all, two of the most widely used ways not only inhibit the assessment or evaluation of E_3 but actually contribute to its commission.

Expert Consensus

In Expert Consensus, truth is not only the product of group consensus, but in addition, the stronger the consensus, the stronger the truth. For example, a particular group's judgment (Democrats, Republicans, Independents) as to who will be the best president of the United States is for all intents and purposes its truth.

E_3 cannot be assessed through this way of thinking because the assumption underlying it is that truth is singular. This way typically does not produce multiple views of problems. Instead, it converges on what a particular group believes best represents the truth of a situation. More often than not, the result is group-think.

Expert Modeling

In Expert Modeling, truth is the set of fundamental assumptions or basic beliefs of an expert community. In turn, the beliefs are generally used to construct a mathematical model of some situation, which is also regarded as the truth.

This way of approaching truth is often used in everyday life. For example, pro-life advocates accept as a fundamental philosophical tenet that a fetus is a person. For them, this belief is so obvious that it is beyond dispute and, as a result, cannot be undermined by any factual experience, such as what happens to the fetus after it is born; whether the parents are married, want the child, can give it a quality upbringing; and so on. All such facts are irrelevant. (For the record, pro-choice advocates can be equally dogmatic.)

As with Expert Consensus, Expert Modeling also typically fails to produce alternative views of problems. Thus, E_3 cannot be assessed in this model. In addition, it can foster E_3.

Multiple Models

Multiple Models lets us begin to assess E_3. In this way of thinking, we *explicitly and deliberately produce multiple views of a problem.* Users of this way believe that decision makers dealing with important problems need to witness explicitly different views before they can decide which version of a problem to pursue.

The different scientific disciplines and professions typically produce different explanations of a phenomenon. Consider, for instance, drug addiction. An economist can define the problem, and hence seek a solution, in terms of the supply and demand of drugs, the various costs to society, the cost of treatment programs, whether the government ought to make drugs available cost-free, and so on. A psychologist, on the other hand, can define the problem in terms of self-esteem, personality disorders, and so on; a sociologist, in terms of the breakdown of the family and societal values; a medical doctor, in terms of physiological processes. Each of these representations is both right and wrong: right in that the variables of a particular discipline or profession do explain part of the problem and wrong in that each is a partial explanation at best.

Because Multiple Models produces a number of distinct views of a problem, we can thereby assess E_3. How good the assessment is depends upon the range of different views that are presented to the decision makers.

Conflict

In the Conflict way of reasoning, *we deliberately and systematically construct at least two different views of an important problem that are the strongest possible opponents of one another.* Only by being exposed to an intensive debate between two or more very different views of an important problem will a decision maker understand the assumptions underlying a particular formulation of a problem.

The case of the Census Bureau discussed in chapter 8 shows the practical application of this way of reasoning. Decision makers can construct practical management processes to explore radically different definitions of problems before taking the critical leap of exploring one in depth and, hence, of getting locked into only one formulation.

The ability to assess E_3 emerges fully only with the use of Conflict. Indeed, we could say that the true purpose of the Conflict way of reasoning is to allow a decision maker to assess E_3. For instance, pro-choice and pro-life positions do not exist in a vacuum. They depend on one another for their existence and their meaning. One position cannot be fully understood by itself, rather only within the context of its contrast with its opposite.

Systemic Reasoning

The Systemic way of reasoning is in many ways a model of models. The Systemic way or model contends that each of the previous four ways or models is appropriate depending on the situation. *We can use the first two general ways for building detailed and precise scientific models of problems, as well as for deriving exact solutions to them, but only after we have used the third and the fourth ways to pick what we regard as an important problem and to decide on its formulation.*

Unlike Expert Consensus and Expert Modeling, the Systemic way does not believe that the scientific disciplines and professions can be arrayed hierarchically from the most important or most rigorous down to the least important or least rigorous. The Systemic way posits that there is not a most important discipline. Because a discipline or profession, say physics, is more rigorous along certain lines does not necessarily make it better or more important than other fields, such as law, which are inherently qualitative. Indeed, the Systemic way shows how all fields of knowledge are inherently interdependent. In this sense, the Systemic way is both a product of and in tune with the Systems Age. In

Expert Consensus and Expert Modeling are products of and hence best suited to the problems of the pre–Machine Age and the Machine Age proper.

fact, Expert Consensus and Expert Modeling are products of and hence best suited to the problems of the pre–Machine Age and the Machine Age proper.

If we regard each scientific discipline as a particular kind of "modeling language," then within the Systemic way each and every language is legitimate. In some cases, one language may be more appropriate than others, but in principle, each is relevant to the description of any problem. Thus, the Systemic way is basic for addressing the importance of language in formulating any problem. In essence, it says no particular language has priority over any other. This helps avoid the E_3, discussed in chapter 5, in which education and professional background affect the terms used to phrase a problem.

The Systemic way poses an enormous challenge to all problem solvers. The two methods that were described in the last chapter for producing dramatically different views of important problems come primarily from two disciplines or professions: (1) psychology and (2) strategic management. In principle, however, *every* discipline and profession has a contribution to make to the multiple representation of important problems. The challenge of the future, therefore, is to continually develop new methods from every discipline and profession of viewing the problems that arise.

Blockers

In addition to the ways in which we think—the ways we use to formulate problems—the most serious obstacles to overcoming E_3 are the overt and covert blockers that individuals, institutions, and even societies put in the way of assessing and managing E_3.

The Systemic way is helpful in understanding such obstacles. It not only helps us understand the nature of individual blockers but, even more important, how blockers interact to form a system in themselves. To reiterate, the individual blockers are not only powerful in themselves, but they become even more powerful when they form a system that blocks our understanding of the broader context in which all problems exist.

It would take a whole book to deal adequately with the varieties of mechanisms that block our abilities to deal effectively with problems, so we will examine one prominent mechanism that operates at the level of a whole industry.

The Divorce between Problem Formulation and Ethics

In earlier chapters, I illustrated how arguments and taken-for-granted assumptions are major contributing factors to E_3. As part of living and working in Los Angeles, I literally cannot count the number of times that I have heard the same set of rationalizations used over and over again at parties and in meetings to justify movie/television violence. Once again, the particular arguments that are most often used are part of a larger fabric.

Mediascope is a Los Angeles–based organization that is funded by, among others, the Carnegie Corporation to study ways of sensitizing Hollywood executives to the effects of television and movie violence. Mediascope also exists to encourage Hollywood executives to develop stories that are less injurious to children. In conjunction with Mediascope, I was a participant in a series of workshops designed to assess the systemic influence of movie/television violence in American society. In effect, an ecological lens was used to estimate the total costs and impacts of violence on American society as a whole.

A major part of the exercise involved determining who lost and who profited from violence. If we consider, for example, the home and industrial security business, the insurance industry, and others, a strong case can be made that a significant part of the U.S. economy profits from violence, and certainly from the fear it engenders.[2]

At a critical point in our discussions, we turned to the arguments that Hollywood executives use frequently to justify their portrayal and general use of violence in films and television. To stand any hope of changing the portrayal and use of violence, it was vital that we get at the underlying beliefs driving the behavior of the industry. For this reason, we tried to list as many arguments as we could think of that, from the experience of the workshop participants, Hollywood executives use to justify their behavior. The list we generated is shown in figure 9-1; the order in which the arguments are listed reflects no significance.

This list is remarkable. It is an incredible mixture of truths, half-truths, distortions, and outright falsehoods. Also, the sheer number of arguments is significant in and of itself. It is a clear indicator of the strength of denial in the industry.

One rarely has the opportunity to see, in a single location, the major rationalizations, or better yet the major defense mechanisms, of an entire industry.[3] This list dispels one of the biggest myths associated with all industries and organizations, namely, that they are uncreative. This is not

1. Direct, causal linkages between (a) violence in films and television and (b) reality have not been established.

2. One cannot measure the "violence content" of a work by merely counting the number of violent acts frame by frame; to do so leads to an inappropriate assessment of the overall "spirit" of a production.

3. Violence has a cathartic effect.

4. Violence is protected under the First Amendment, i.e., under freedom of expression.

5. Humans are predisposed to violence.

6. If there is only a small group that is especially predisposed to violence, why then does the media have to be responsible for a fringe group?

7. Violence is largely due to the widespread availability of guns in our society; therefore, the elimination of violence is someone else's problem or another force in society.

8. Violence is justified under artistic expression.

9. The public wants violence as shown by ratings and box office receipts.

10. There is a small repeat audience for violent films; not everyone wants them, but those who do come back in numbers.

11. People are inherently and naturally violent; violence is part of the human condition.

12. Violence has always been a form of entertainment.

13. Violence not only sells but, hence, keeps my job.

14. Violence not only sells, but it translates well across cultural barriers.

15. Drugs and the breakup of the family are bigger contributors to the violence in society than films and television.

16. I grew up on violence, and my kids as well, but we are not violent.

17. The audience knows that it's just a fantasy on the screen; hence, it can differentiate between fantasy and reality.

18. Parents should take responsibility for what their children watch.

19. The rating system itself is sufficient protection for young children.

20. Children should not be up late at night in order to watch adult programming; hence, the hours of the day are themselves a protection.

21. There is an "aesthetics of violence" that is similar to the aesthetics of dance; hence, one can view "violence" in other terms.

Figure 9-1   Arguments Used to Justify Television and Movie Violence

22. Violence can be pro-social; violence is supposed to be upsetting.

23. The essence of drama is conflict; drama often needs to be violent in order to raise it to greater heights.

24. Violence is more connected with poverty than it is with films or television.

25. Violence is learned in the family.

26. Art merely reflects society, or holds up a mirror to it; art does not create society.

27. The media often are only portraying "real stories"; what is shown is based on true news stories.

28. Violence is to be found throughout all world literature such as fairy tales, Greek myths, Shakespeare, the Bible, Grimm's Fairy Tales; in fact, these sources are much more violent than anything that is shown on television or in films.

29. Japanese films are far more violent than American films, yet Japanese society is not as violent as American.

30. Some groups are inherently more violent than others; this is not our problem.

31. The general deterioration of society leads to violence.

32. Violence and deterioration are in fact the natural course of things; all societies appear to deteriorate and spiral down.

33. The general lack of discipline in schools and by parents is the major contributing factor to increased violence.

34. The general audience is too stupid to accept complex stories; hence, we are forced to use violence.

35. The decision to produce a particular story is made on a strict commercial/business basis, not on the use of violence per se.

36. Those actors who appear regularly in action/adventure films command more money.

37. The audience now wants to see women in aggressive/violent roles to counter the stereotypical roles in which they have been portrayed in the past.

38. Violence is a major theme in all art; violence overcomes evil; it represents the perpetual struggle of good over evil.

39. Violence is part of the warrior archetype; it represents the struggle of the hero and even the anti-hero.

only a false myth but a dangerous one. All industries and organizations are creative; the issue is where that creativity is directed. In the case of the tobacco industry, much of its creativity is directed toward the production of dangerous products and a dysfunctional system of beliefs that justifies those products, such as "Smoking is an individual right and there is no conclusive evidence that smoking *causes* cancer."

Hollywood is another such industry, and like many organizations and industries, it is split, if not downright schizoid. It produces a wealth of movies and television shows that are creative, educational, entertaining, and morally uplifting. It also supports a number of worthy causes, such as benefits for AIDS patients and AIDS research and protection of the physical environment. At the same time, it produces products that are distasteful at best and highly injurious, if not outright unethical, at worst.

Only by being exposed to an intensive debate between two or more very different views of an important problem will a decision maker understand the assumptions underlying a particular formulation of a problem.

Figure 9-1 exhibits another significant characteristic of E_3: it is rooted firmly in denial. For this reason, figure 9-1 is overwhelming. Denial is never content with one justification; if it were, it would not be denial. Denial always works by overkill. At some level, the mind of a single individual, or the collective mind of an institution, always knows that what is being defended is patently false. While there are no exact formulas, precisely because the unconscious does not work in that way, the number of rationalizations is an indicator of the strength of denial.[4] It is also an indicator that the industry is more interested in putting its creative energies into denial than into the production of television programs and movies that do not depend on violence for attracting and retaining viewers.

The fundamental underlying blocker in the above example—as well as many others discussed in this book—is the divorce between problem formulation and ethics and, more generally, between ethics and management. By denying that there is a problem, or that it is part of the problem, the movie/television industry does not have to participate in the solution.

The Metaphysics of Management

In chapter 1 we discussed the four steps of the problem-solving process: (1) acknowledgment or recognition of the existence of a problem, (2) formulation of the problem, (3) derivation of the solution to the problem, and (4) implementation of the solution. E_3 can happen during any one of the four steps.

This book has primarily discussed the second step, formulation of the problem, but step four, implementation, deserves a special word. As the philosopher C. West Churchman has so astutely noted, academics and intellectuals in general believe that our job, the hard work of problem solving, is finished once we have formulated a theoretical definition of a problem and extracted a solution to it. This view is not only naive but dangerous.

Even though I have spent virtually all of my academic career in business schools, I unfortunately, like so many of my university colleagues, have regarded management as a tenth-rate discipline at best. As noted earlier, I believe that social scientists generally suffer from "physics envy." However, as we have been realizing the weight of the issues connected with human management, C. West Churchman and I have come to believe that management is a discipline of first-rate importance.[5] Compared to the problems of management, physics problems are easy, if not trivial. For instance, the implementation of the solution to important problems is one of the most difficult of all human activities. This type of research is not over once the ideal solution to some problem has been found. The real problem, managing the implementation of the solution, is only just beginning.

Ethical Management

Everything that humans do involves an aspect of management. William James, one of the most important and original of all philosophers, came tantalizingly close to understanding this, although he didn't quite. According to his theory of pragmatism, truth is that which makes a *significant difference* in human affairs. For Churchman and myself, truth is that which makes an *ethical difference* in human affairs, that is, leads to the betterment of the human condition.[6]

Although James defined truth as that which makes a difference, he did not give much attention to the *process* by which that difference is made. Further, like so many intellectuals, James considered science to be the basis for knowledge, superior to all other forms of inquiry. Science was thereby the process by which one achieved truth. In contrast, for Churchman and myself, truth begins to result only when we are able to make significant differences in the management of human affairs.

Let me contrast the two approaches by quoting from James's *Pragmatism:*

> The truth of an idea is not a stagnant property inherent in it. *Truth happens* to an idea. It *becomes true,* is *made true* by events. Its verity *is* in fact an event, a process: the process mainly

of its verifying itself, its veri-*fication*. Its validity is the process of its vali-*dation*. [James's emphasis.][7]

In contrast, our notion of truth is founded on the fundamental importance of implementation and management. Thus, Churchman and I would reword James's ideas as follows:

> The truth of a scientific finding (fact), or an idea, is not a static property inherent in it. Truth *happens* as a result of the ethical management of human affairs. It *becomes true, is discovered*, and *made true* by ethical actions. Its verity *is* in fact a series of ethical actions, a process: the process of its *ethical implementation*. Its validity is gained through what may generally be called "*the management of truth*."

E_3 does not cease to exist once we have chosen the right definition of a problem, or even after we have derived the right solution to the right definition. E_3 ceases to exist only after we have *implemented* the right solution to the right definition of an important problem.

If we have not included the implementation of the solution in a problem's initial definition, then we have not correctly defined the problem in the first place. Furthermore, if we can't define a problem so that it leads to ethical actions that benefit humankind, then either we haven't defined or are currently unable to define the problem properly.

A Spiritual Breakthrough?

There is no question that in many respects humankind is still primitive with regard to problem solving. For this reason, a real breakthrough is needed before we can define many of our most important problems properly, let alone solve them.

Many of the definitions of our most important problems, and certainly what we take as solutions, are best viewed as addictions. For instance, some of us are addicted to Machine Age thinking, management fads, and anything else that keeps us from thinking systemically and ethically. Thus, changing how we approach problems is akin to breaking long-standing addictions.

One of the very few interventions of which I am aware that has been successful in treating serious addictions is Alcoholics Anonymous (AA), although it also is not without limitations. The traditional Twelve Steps of

AA are given in figure 9-2. I say traditional with reservations, since the steps are intended to have as many interpretations as there are persons who are in need of AA. If the steps are not only to take on meaning but to restore meaning to the lives of addicts, then there must be a *management process* through which the steps are continually reinterpreted so that they continue to apply to an addict's life.

The Twelve Steps of AA are not only a general management system for the explicit purpose of treating serious addictions, but they also constitute a very special management system whose most prominent feature is its emphasis on spirituality. The fundamental assumption of AA is that the disease from which an addict is suffering is a loss of meaning and purpose. In short, the addict's basic problem is one of spiritual emptiness, hence, the constant emphasis on God or one's Higher Power throughout *all* of the Twelve Steps. This does not mean that there is only one correct interpretation of God or one's Higher Power. One of the most important features of AA is the freedom it gives to each individual to interpret one's Higher Power as one conceives of it. In effect, AA is a religion without official priests, a therapy without official therapists.

The Twelve Steps are governed by a constant emphasis on taking a moral assessment, or ethical evaluation, with regard to all the parties, or stakeholders, that one has hurt in the past through addiction to alcohol, drugs, gambling, guns, power, or whatever it may be. The system is also characterized by its constant emphasis on taking action, that is, ethical implementation, in order to treat the addict and his or her surrounding social system. Thus, while not perfect, as no management system is, the Twelve Steps are an important blend of ethics, implementation, and spirituality.

The Systemic way of reasoning is in many ways a model of models.

Twelve-Step Procedure for Spiritual Management

Current academic and popular literature on management contains endless discussions of countless variables that supposedly lead to effective management. For the most part, these variables are cognitive, intellectual, or structural (for example, an organization's reward system). Virtually none of the discussions make any mention of aesthetics, ethics, existential needs, or spirituality as important variables, let alone as significant management problems.

True, discussions on the importance of spirituality in management are appearing. However, for the most part, these are outside the mainstream.[8]

1. We admitted we were powerless over alcohol, that our lives had become unmanageable.

2. Came to believe that a Power greater than ourselves could restore us to sanity.

3. Made a decision to turn our will and our lives over to the care of God as we understood Him.

4. Made a searching and fearless moral inventory of ourselves.

5. Admitted to God, to ourselves, and to another human being the exact nature of our wrongs.

6. Were entirely ready to have God remove all these defects of character.

7. Humbly asked Him to remove our shortcomings.

8. Made a list of all persons we had harmed and became willing to make amends to them all.

9. Made direct amends to such people wherever possible except when to do so would injure them or others.

10. Continued to take personal inventory and when we were wrong promptly admitted it.

11. Sought through prayer and meditation to improve our conscious contact with God as we understood Him, praying only for the knowledge of His will for us and the power to carry that out.

12. Having had a spiritual awakening as a result of these steps, we try to carry this message to alcoholics, and to practice these principles in all our affairs.

Source: Alcoholics Anonymous, 1957

Figure 9-2   Twelve Steps

Thus, I would offer this bold assertion: *To the extent that virtually none of the major theories of management explicitly incorporate aesthetics, ethics, existential needs, and spirituality as among the most important concerns of human beings, we have no comprehensive theories of management!*

An even more radical challenge to conventional management follows: Truth is spiritual to the extent that it demands that we engage in a continual, ongoing process to redesign our lives to *remove the blockages to the ethical implementation of ethical ideas*. To my knowledge, the degree of lifelong ethical and spiritual involvement that I see as necessary to truth is not present in today's management or science.

Throughout this book, I have deliberately avoided giving an exact or precise definition of spirituality, since that definition means little apart from a program of continually rebuilding an individual's or an organization's life. The definition of spirituality in this context is one of the primary purposes of the Twelve Steps of AA. Thus, the Twelve Steps can be construed as a management process for defining spirituality, but only within the total context of an individual's or an organization's life and the process of giving new and revitalized meaning to that life.

Spirituality is an integral part, if not the very essence, of management. It entails treating all of the stakeholders connected with a business with caring, concern, and dignity. This further entails the three ethical imperatives: (1) products and services ought to be ethical to begin with; (2) products and services ought to be made available to all who have an ethical need of them with minimal profits to the organization producing them; and (3) an organization has a deep responsibility to foster development and recovery of all its stakeholders, such as employees, families, surrounding communities, and so on.

This last ethical imperative rests on the notion that organizations cannot be competitive, even in a traditional economic sense, when their employees and top management are emotionally unhealthy.

Since the vast majority of today's organizations are deeply dysfunctional, I believe with others that AA needs to be extended to organizations.[9] Like alcoholics, many of today's organizations exhibit behaviors akin to those found in dysfunctional families: denial; dishonesty; faulty reasoning processes; psychological, physical, and sexual abuse; and so on. For this reason, many—perhaps most—organizations cannot be changed merely through rational or cognitive programs. They require programs of deep recovery that are akin to AA. In short, it is a fundamental tenet of spiritual management that organizations, like individuals, need to be in continual and ongoing programs of treatment and recovery. Existential concerns, spirituality, and recovery are central to organizations, not peripheral or secondary.

Conclusion

It would be the height of arrogance and naiveté to think that the mere concept of E_3, by itself, would lead automatically to both the formulation of the right problems and the will to work on them. I harbor no such illusions. If anything, I wish that today's academics and management consultants had the honesty of the greatest mathematicians and physicists, who have never hesitated to admit that they don't know how to formulate certain problems, let alone how to solve them. Such an admission is neither a statement of defeat nor of hopelessness; it is a call to work harder.

In the end, I believe strongly that faulty definitions retard seriously our abilities to solve important problems. For instance, the hackneyed expression "Guns don't kill people; people kill people" is wrong because a better statement of the issue is "People kill people *more effectively* by means of guns than they do by other means."

We circle back to where we began. How can we better formulate the problem of formulating problems?

Critical Questions for You and Your Organization

1. Which of the five ways of thinking described in this chapter do you and your organization typically adopt? Why?

2. Make a list of the blockers that prevent you and your organization from defining problems. How can these blockers be overcome?

3. How could the principles of AA, either singly or in combination, be applied to your organization?

Notes

Preface

1. John Dewey, *The Quest for Certainty* (New York: G. P. Putnam, 1928).

Chapter 1

1. Louis Sahagun, "Boy's Bear Hunt Wish Puts Foundation in Cross Hairs, Animal Activists Up in Arms at Make-A-Wish for Allowing Dying Teenager to Kill a Kodiac in Alaska," *Los Angeles Times*, 11 May 1996.

Chapter 2

1. For a somewhat dated but still excellent text, see Harold Freeman, *Introduction to Statistical Inference* (Reading, Mass: Addison-Wesley, 1963).

2. In Howard Raiffa, *Decision Analysis* (Reading, Mass: Addison-Wesley, 1968), 264, the eminent decision theorist Howard Raiffa describes his first contact with the Error of the Third Kind:

   In my first operations research problem, I fell into the trap of working on a wrong problem. One of the most popular paradigms in the theory of mathematics describes the case in which a researcher has either to accept or reject a so-called null hypothesis. In a first course in Statistics the student learns that he must constantly balance between making an error of the first kind (that is, rejecting the null hypothesis when it is true), and an error of the second kind (that is, accepting the null hypothesis when it is false). I believe it was John Tukey who suggested that practitioners all too often commit an error of a third kind: solving the wrong problem.

3. See Raiffa, *Decision Analysis*.

4. John Thor Dahlburg, "In India Ad World, Hitler Can Mean Fun," *Los Angeles Times*, 14 October 1994.

5. Robert Welkos, "Gee, It Sounded Like a Good Idea, 'Cute' Real Estate Ad in the Hollywood Reporter Generates Complaints," *Los Angeles Times*, 12 March 1994.

6. Susan Byrnes, "Billboards Draw Ire of Cancer Patients, Popeye's Chicken Orders Signs Taken Down after Complaints That an Intended Joke Is Offensive," *Los Angeles Times,* 27 April 1994.

7. Ian I. Mitroff, Christine M. Pearson, and L. Katharine Harrington, *The Essential Guide to Managing Corporate Crises: A Step-by-Step Handbook for Surviving Major Catastrophes* (New York: Oxford University Press, 1996).

8. See Ian I. Mitroff and Harold A. Linstone, *The Unbounded Mind* (New York: Oxford University Press, 1993).

9. See Mitroff and Linstone, *The Unbounded Mind.*

10. Mitroff, Pearson, and Harrington, *The Essential Guide.*

11. Richard C. Paddock, "Critics Mobilize an Effort to Block Ocean Noise Test," *Los Angeles Times,* 23 March 1994; Richard C. Paddock, "Scientists Defend Ocean Noise Tests," *Los Angeles Times,* 24 March 1994.

12. See Ian I. Mitroff and Thierry C. Pauchant, *We're So Big and Powerful Nothing Bad Can Happen to Us: An Investigation of America's Crisis-Prone Corporations* (New York: Birch Lane Press, 1990).

13. Katharine Q. Seelye, "Dole Depicts Himself As Tougher on Crime and Criminals Than the President," *New York Times,* 12 May 1996.

Chapter 3

1. See Heinz Kohut, *The Analysis of the Self: A Systematic Approach to the Psychoanalytic Treatment of Narcissistic Disorders* (New York: International University Press, 1971). See also H. Kohut, *The Restoration of Self* (New York: International University Press, 1977).

2. Michael Quinn, *Time,* 8 May 1995, 38.

3. See Joshua Meyrowitz, *No Sense of Place: The Impact of Electronic Media on Social Behavior* (New York: Oxford University Press, 1985).

4. Robert Hartley, *Marketing Mistakes* (New York: John Wiley, 1992).

Chapter 4

1. For more technical descriptions and formulations of the Type III Error, see Ian I. Mitroff and Frederick Betz, "Dialectical Decision Theory: A Meta-Theory of Decision Making," *Management Science* 19, no. 1 (1972): 11–24; Ian I. Mitroff and Tom R. Featheringham, "On Systemic Problem Solving and the Error of the Third Kind," *Behavioral Science* 19, no. 6 (1974): 383–393; see also Ian I. Mitroff and Ralph Kilmann, *Methodological Approaches to Social Science* (San Francisco: Jossey-Bass Publishers Inc., 1978).

2. Ian I. Mitroff, *The Subjective Side of Science: A Philosophical Inquiry into the Psychology of the Apollo Moon Scientists* (Amsterdam: Elsevier, 1974).

3. For a discussion of "soul" and its place within business, see Alan Briskin, *The Stirring of Soul in the Work Place* (San Francisco: Jossey-Bass, 1996).

4. See Briskin, *The Stirring of Soul.*

Chapter 5

1. Robert M. May, "How Many Species Inhabit the Earth?" *Scientific American* (October 1992): 42–48.

2. Ibid.

3. L. Rowell Husemann and Leonard D. Eron, eds., *Television and the Aggressive Child: A Cross-National Comparison* (Hillsdale, N.J.: Lawrence Earlbaum Associates, 1986).

4. Alexander Cockburn, "Real Blood Isn't Shed in the Movies, Kids Learn Violence as the Victims of Battering by Grown-Ups, Not from Hollywood," *Los Angeles Times,* 19 May 1996.

5. The Constitutional objection is an interesting one, which shows that the movie/television and legal industries are willing both to deny and to use causality when it suits their purposes. The correlations between movie/TV and real-world violence are not high enough to meet the law's exacting demands when it comes to limiting speech on the grounds that it poses a "*clear and present* [read, *causal*] danger to the welfare of children." On the other hand, those who oppose any restraints on speech—assuming "violence" is speech—(see Katharine A. MacKinnon, *Only Words* [Cambridge, Mass: Harvard University Press, 1993]) assert that violence often produces a cathartic effect that "calms" those who watch it. Even though this claim is false (see Irenaus Eibl-Eibesfeldt, *The Biology of Peace and War: Men, Animals, and Aggression* [New York: Viking Press, 1975]), it is nonetheless a "causal" claim in disguise [namely, "violence calms"] on the part of those who use causality when it suits them.

6. Thomas Moore, *The Education of the Heart* (New York: HarperCollins, 1996), 43.

Chapter 6

1. See Ian I. Mitroff, Richard O. Mason, and Christine Pearson, *Framebreak, The Radical Redesign of American Business* (San Francisco: Jossey-Bass, 1994).

2. Alvin Toffler, *Power Shift: Knowledge, Wealth, and Violence at the Edge of the Twenty-First Century* (New York: Bantam Books, 1990), 185, 212.

3. Peter Senge, *The Fifth Discipline* (New York: Doubleday Dell, 1990); Michael Hammer and James Champy, *Re-engineering the Corporation* (New York: Harper and Row, 1993).

4. Daniel J. Boorstein, *The Discoverers: A History of Man's Search to Know His World and Himself* (New York: Vintage Books, 1983).

5. See, for instance, Joshua Meyrowitz, *No Sense of Place: The Impact of Electronic Media on Social Behavior* (New York: Oxford University Press, 1985); see also

Ian I. Mitroff and Warren Bennis, *The Unreality Industry* (New York: Oxford University Press, 1989).

6. Alvin Toffler, *Future Shock* (New York: Bantam Books, 1971).

7. The poisoning of Tylenol, perhaps the most notorious and famous case of product tampering, shows how powerful the urge is to deny vulnerabilities and, as a result, to avoid thinking about the unthinkable. Early in September 1982, at the annual three-day Strategic Planning Retreat of Johnson and Johnson, the parent company of McNeil Pharmaceuticals, makers of Tylenol, J&J's chairman, James Burke, mused at how lucky they were to be in an industry that had such extremely profitable brands. However, he reflected out loud, "What if something happened to one of [our main products], like Tylenol? Nothing," he noted, "is impregnable." Not only could no one come up with anything that could dampen what seemed to be an extraordinarily successful business, but Burke "took some kidding . . . for worrying about things [he didn't] have to."

Unfortunately, the unthinkable occurred. On September 29, 1982, two brothers, Adam and Steven Janus, and Mary Kellerman, of two different suburbs outside of Chicago, died from taking Extra Strength Tylenol capsules. Cyanide, a deadly poison, had been injected into the capsules. See Thomas Moore, "The Fight to Save Tylenol," *Fortune,* 29 November 1982, 44–49; see also Ian I. Mitroff and Ralph H. Kilmann, *Corporate Tragedies: Product Tampering, Sabotage, and Other Catastrophes* (New York: Praeger, 1984).

8. See Russell Ackoff, *Creating the Corporate Future* (New York: John Wiley, 1981).

9. See Ian I. Mitroff and Harold A. Linstone, *The Unbounded Mind* (New York: Oxford University Press, 1993).

10. Ackoff, *Creating the Corporate Future.*

11. Ibid.

12. See Russell L. Ackoff, *The Democratic Organization, A Radical Prescription Recreating Corporate America and Rediscovering Success* (New York: Oxford University Press, 1994); see also the excellent article by Wayne F. Cascio, "Downsizing: What Do We Know? What Have We Learned?" *The Executive* 7, no. 1 (February 1993): 95–104.

13. Cascio, "Downsizing"; see Garry D. Bruton et al., "Downsizing the Firm: Answering the Strategic Questions," *Academy of Management Executives* 10, no. 2 (1996): 38–45.

14. Brian A. Lt., "Chaparral Steel: Unleash Workers and Cut Costs," *Fortune,* 18 May 1992, 88.

15. Ian I. Mitroff, Christine M. Pearson, and L. Katharine Harrington, *The Essential Guide to Managing Corporate Crises: A Step-by-Step Handbook for Surviving Major Catastrophes* (New York: Oxford University Press, 1996).

Chapter 7

1. Pamela Sherrid, "Tampons after the Shock Wave," *Fortune,* 10 August 1981, 114–129.

2. "Tampons, Not Relied On," *The Economist,* 27 September 1980, 100.

3. Sherrid, "Tampons after the Shock Wave," 115.

4. "Toxic Shock, Horror Mystery," *The Economist,* 18 October 1980, 42.

5. Ibid.

6. Edward Tenner, *Why Things Bite Back: Technology and the Revenge of Unintended Consequences* (New York: Alfred A. Knopf, 1996).

7. Given the awesome destructive power of nuclear weapons, those who should have known better engaged in pernicious arguments nonetheless, and as a result, committed an E_3; see Henry Kissinger, *Nuclear Weapons and Foreign Policy* (New York: Norton Library, 1969) for an example of this type of E_3. One of the most serious issues connected with nuclear war was how to keep it from escalating once it started. Henry Kissinger argued that given the immense power of nuclear weapons, if a nuclear war broke out, then both sides would have to behave exceedingly rationally and calmly in order to keep the situation from getting further out of hand. Kissinger's argument is truly incredible! If rationality and calmness could prevail, why then did the two sides get into war in the first place, let alone a nuclear one? Further, if rationality and calmness were not present *before* a war started, how then would they suddenly appear *later* in the heat of actual battle, where human powers are stressed to their limit? Even so-called "brilliant minds" are thus perfectly capable of uttering and defending lame positions.

8. Sun Tzu, *The Art of War,* edited by James Clavell (New York: Delacorte Press, 1983).

9. See Ian I. Mitroff, "The Complete and Utter Failure of Traditional Thinking in Comprehending the Nuclear Predicament: Why It's Impossible to Formulate a Paradox-Free Theory of Nuclear Policy," *Journal of Technological Forecasting and Social Change* 29 (1976): 51–72.

10. See Robert Jervis, *The Illogic of American Nuclear Strategy* (Ithaca, N.Y.: Cornell University Press, 1984). Although it comes tantalizingly close to the analysis developed in this book, Jervis's excellent book does not carry the notion of paradox and contradiction as deeply and as pervasively as I do. What Jervis calls the "tension" inherent in traditional notions of deterrence I believe is better captured by the concept of dialectical contradiction. My position is thus much more extreme than his. This does not detract either from the cogency of his arguments or from the overall excellence of his book.

11. See Robert F. Hartley, *Marketing Mistakes* (New York: John Wiley & Sons, 1992).

12. See Ian I. Mitroff and Harold A. Linstone, *The Unbounded Mind* (New York: Oxford University Press, 1993).

13. E. F. Schumacher, *Small Is Beautiful: Economics As If People Mattered* (New York: Harper & Row, 1973).

14. See Susan Haack, *Deviant Logic: Some Philosophical Issues* (Cambridge: Cambridge University Press, 1974).

15. Amy Harmon, "Surging Internet Use Strains Phone System," *Los Angeles Times,* 31 October 1996.

16. Ronald Hankoff, "Growing Your Company: Five Ways to Do It Right!" *Fortune,* 25 November 1996, 78–79, 88.

17. Russell L. Ackoff, *Creating the Corporate Future: Plan or Be Planned For* (New York: John Wiley & Sons, 1981).

Chapter 8

1. See Harold S. Kushner, *How Good Do We Have to Be? A New Understanding of Guilt and Forgiveness* (New York: Little, Brown, and Company, 1996).

2. See Richard O. Mason and Ian I. Mitroff, *Challenging Strategic Planning Assumptions* (New York: John Wiley, 1981).

3. Carl Jung, *Volume 6, Psychological Types* (Princeton, N.J.: Princeton University Press, 1955).

4. Ibid.

5. Ibid.

6. Isabel Briggs Myers, *Gifts Differing* (Palo Alto, Calif.: Consulting Psychologists Press, Inc., 1980).

7. Ian I. Mitroff and Harold A. Linstone, *The Unbounded Mind* (New York: Oxford University Press, 1993).

8. See Ian I. Mitroff, Richard O. Mason, and Vincent P. Barabba, *The 1980 Census: Policy Making amid Turbulence* (Lexington, Mass.: Lexington Books, 1983).

9. Ibid.

10. Gerald Zaltman and Vincent P. Barabba, *Hearing the Voice of the Market* (Cambridge: Harvard Business School Press, 1991).

Chapter 9

1. Ian I. Mitroff and Harold A. Linstone, *The Unbounded Mind* (New York: Oxford University Press, 1993).

2. Judy Pasternak, "Profiting Off the Frightened," *Los Angeles Times,* 17 December 1994.

3. See Thierry C. Pauchant and Ian I. Mitroff, *Transforming the Crisis Prone Organization* (San Francisco: Jossey-Bass Inc. Publishers, 1992).

4. Ibid.

5. C. West Churchman, personal communication.

6. Ibid.

7. William James, *Pragmatism* (Buffalo, N.Y.: Prometheus Books, 1991), 89.

8. See L. G. Bolman and T. E. Deal, *Leading with Soul: An Uncommon Journey of Spirit* (San Francisco: Jossey-Bass, 1995); see also J. A. Conger and Associates, *Spirit at Work: Discovering the Spirituality in Leadership* (San Francisco: Jossey-Bass, 1994); see also I. I. Mitroff, R. O. Mason, and C. M. Pearson, *Framebreak: The Radical Redesign of American Business* (San Francisco: Jossey-Bass, 1994).

9. A. W. Schaef and D. Fassel, *The Addictive Organization: Why We Overwork, Cover Up, Pick Up the Pieces, Please the Boss, and Perpetuate Sick Organizations* (New York: Harper Collins, 1988). See also L. Robbins, "Designing More Functional Organizations: The Twelve-Step Model," *The Journal of Organizational Change Management* 5 (1993): 4–22.

Index

About the Author

Ian I. Mitroff is the Harold Quinton Distinguished Professor of Business Policy and the Founder of the University of Southern California Center for Crisis Management, which he directed for ten years at the Graduate School of Business, University of Southern California, Los Angeles. He is also the president of Comprehensive Crisis Management, a private consulting firm in Manhattan Beach, California.

He received his B.S. in Engineering Physics, his M.S. in Structural Engineering, and his Ph.D. in Engineering Science and the Philosophy of Social Science, all from the University of California at Berkeley.

He has been a professor of business administration, information science, and sociology and a research associate at the Philosophy of Science Center at the University of Pittsburgh. He has also been a visiting professor in the departments of Management and Social Systems Sciences at the Wharton School, University of Pennsylvania.

He is a Fellow of the American Psychological Association and the Academy of Management.

He has published over two hundred and fifty articles and nineteen books. He writes frequent op-ed pieces for leading newspapers and is a frequent guest on *Marketplace* on National Public Radio.

He consults widely on crisis management, critical thinking, organizational and strategic change, and strategic planning for a wide array of public and private organizations.

He is currently completing one of the first systematic studies of spirituality in the workplace.

Berrett-Koehler Publishers

BERRETT-KOEHLER is an independent publisher of books, periodicals, and other publications at the leading edge of new thinking and innovative practice on work, business, management, leadership, stewardship, career development, human resources, entrepreneurship, and global sustainability.

Since the company's founding in 1992, we have been committed to supporting the movement toward a more enlightened world of work by publishing books, periodicals, and other publications that help us to integrate our values with our work and work lives, and to create more humane and effective organizations.

We have chosen to focus on the areas of work, business, and organizations, because these are central elements in many people's lives today. Furthermore, the work world is going through tumultuous changes, from the decline of job security to the rise of new structures for organizing people and work. We believe that change is needed at all levels— individual, organizational, community, and global—and our publications address each of these levels.

We seek to create new lenses for understanding organizations, to legitimize topics that people care deeply about but that current business orthodoxy censors or considers secondary to bottom-line concerns, and to uncover new meaning, means, and ends for our work and work lives.

See next page for other books from Berrett-Koehler Publishers

Other leading-edge business books
from Berrett-Koehler Publishers

Corporate Tides
The Inescapable Laws of Organizational Structure
Robert Fritz

CORPORATE LEADERS waste billions of dollars each year on attempts to change organizations through programs that were doomed before they started. In *Corporate Tides,* Fritz addresses this dilemma head-on by addressing the fundamental causes of organizational success or failure. He shows that once structural forces are understood and structural principles applied within the organization, managers can achieve real, lasting success for the company.

Hardcover, 200 pages, June 1996 • ISBN 1-881052-88-5

Item no. 52885-235 $27.95

The New Management
Democracy and Enterprise Are Transforming Organizations
William E. Halal

TODAY'S MANAGERS are confronted with a bewildering blur of change, ranging from downsizing to spirituality. *The New Management* cuts through the confusion by integrating emerging practices into a coherent, clarifying whole. Drawing on hundreds of examples from progressive companies, an international survey of 426 managers, and economic trends, William Halal shows how enterprise and democracy are moving inside of business and government to transform institutions for the Information Age.

Hardcover, 204 pages, 5/96 • ISBN 1-881052-53-2 CIP • **Item no. 52532-235 $29.95**

Imagination
New Mindsets for Seeing, Organizing, and Managing
Gareth Morgan

"IMAGINIZATION" is a way of thinking and organizing. It is a key managerial skill that will help you understand and develop your own creative potential, and find innovative solutions to difficult problems. It answers the call for more creative forms of organization and management and shows how we can find new roles in a changing, uncertain world.

Paperback, 350 pages, 8/97 • ISBN 1-57675-026-4 CIP • **Item no. 50264-235**

Available at your favorite bookstore, or call 1-800-929-2929

The Fourth Wave
Business in the 21st Century

Herman Bryant Maynard, Jr. and Susan E. Mehrtens

APPLYING THE CONCEPT of historical waves originally propounded by Alvin Toffler in *The Third Wave,* Herman Maynard and Susan Mehrtens look toward the next century and foresee a "fourth wave," an era of integration and responsibility far beyond Toffler's revolutionary description of third-wave postindustrial society. They examine how business has changed in the second and third waves and must continue to change in the fourth. The changes concern the basics—how an institution is organized, how it defines wealth, how it relates to surrounding communities, how it responds to environmental needs, and how it takes part in the political process.

Paperback, 236 pages, 7/96 • ISBN 1-57675-002-7 • **Item no. 50027-235** **$18.95**
Hardcover, 6/93 • ISBN 1-881052-15-X • **Item no. 5215X-235** **$28.95**

Building a Win-Win World
Life Beyond Global Economic Warfare

Hazel Henderson

WORLD-RENOWNED FUTURIST Hazel Henderson extends her twenty-five years of work in economics to examine the havoc the current economic system is creating at the global level. *Building a Win-Win World* demonstrates how the global economy is unsustainable because of its negative effects on employees, families, communities, and the ecosystem. Henderson shows that win-win strategies can become the norm at every level when people see the true current and future costs of short-sighted, narrow economic policies.

Hardcover, 320 pages, 6/96 • ISBN 1-881052-90-7 • **Item no. 52907-235** **$29.95**
Paperback, 10/97 • ISBN 1-57675-027-2 • **Item no. 50272-235** **$19.95**

When Corporations Rule the World

David C. Korten

DAVID KORTEN offers an alarming exposé of the devastating consequences of economic globalization and a passionate message of hope in this well-reasoned, extensively researched analysis. He documents the human and environmental consequences of economic globalization, and explain why human survival depends on a community-based, people-centered alternative.

Paperback, 384 pages, 9/96 • ISBN 1-887208-01-1 • **Item no. 0801-235** **$19.95**
Hardcover, 9/95 • ISBN 1-887208-00-3 • **Item no. 08003-235** **$29.95**

Available at your favorite bookstore, or call 1-800-929-2929

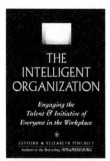

The Intelligent Organization*

Engaging the Talent and Initiative of Everyone in the Workplace

Gifford and Elizabeth Pinchot

THIS BOOK shows how to replace bureaucracy with more humane and effective systems for organizing and coordinating work. Gifford and Elizabeth Pinchot show how, by developing and engaging the intelligence, business judgment, and wide-system responsibility of all its members, an organization can respond more effectively to customers, partners, and competitors.

*Originally published in hardcover with the title *The End of Bureaucracy and the Rise of the Intelligent Organization*

Paperback, 420 pages, 10/96 • ISBN 1-881052-98-2 CIP • **Item no. 52982-235 $19.95**
Hardcover, 3/94 • ISBN 1-881052-34-6 CIP • **Item no. 52346-235 $24.95**

The Age of Participation

New Governance for the Workplace and the World

by Patricia McLagan and Christo Nel

foreword by Peter Block

PATRICIA McLAGAN and Christo Nel describe the massive transformation that is occurring in human institutions today. Blending theory and practice, providing numerous examples, and drawing on more than forty years of experience in over 200 organizations, McLagan and Nel describe what executives, managers, workers, labor unions, customers, and suppliers can do as part of a participative enterprise. In this practical, experience-based handbook, they look closely at every level of life in a participative organization and deflate the fears and misperceptions that can sabotage change.

Hardcover, 340 pages, 9/95 • ISBN 1-881052-56-7 CIP • **Item no. 52567-235 $27.95**
Paperback, 2/97 • ISBN 1-57675-012-4 • **Item no. 50124-235 $18.95**

Stewardship

Choosing Service Over Self-Interest

Peter Block

Peter Block shows how to recreate our workplaces by replacing self-interest, dependency, and control with service, responsibility, and partnership. In this revolutionary book, he demonstrates how a far-reaching redistribution of power, privilege, and wealth will radically change all areas of organizational governance, and shows why this is our best hope to enable democracy to thrive, our spiritual and ethical values to be lived out, and economic success to be sustained.

Paperback, 288 pages, 3/96 • ISBN 1-881052-86-9 CIP • **Item no. 52869-235 $16.95**
Hardcover, 7/93 • ISBN 1-881052-28-1 CIP • **Item no. 52281-235 $27.95**

Available at your favorite bookstore, or call 1-800-929-2929

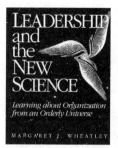

Leadership and the New Science

Learning about Organization from an Orderly Universe

Margaret J. Wheatley

"The Best Management Book of the Year!"
—*Industry Week* magazine survey by Tom Brown

OUR UNDERSTANDING of the universe is being radically altered by the "New Science"—the revolutionary discoveries in quantum physics, chaos theory, and evolutionary biology that are overturning the prevailing models of science. Now, in this pioneering book, Wheatley shows how the new science provides equally powerful insights for changing how we design, lead, manage, and view organizations.

Paperback, 172 pages, 3/94 • ISBN 1-881052-44-3 • **Item no. 52443-235 $15.95**
Hardcover, 9/92 • ISBN 1-881052-01-X • **Item no. 5201X-235 $24.95**

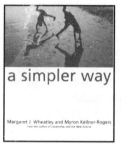

A Simpler Way

Margaret J. Wheatley and Myron Kellner-Rogers

A *SIMPLER WAY* is the widely awaited new book from Margaret J. Wheatley, author of the bestselling *Leadership and the New Science*. Here, Wheatley and coauthor Myron Kellner-Rogers explore the primary question, "How could we organize human endeavor if we developed different understandings of how life organizes itself?" They draw on the work of scientists, philosophers, poets, novelists, spiritual teachers, colleagues, audiences, and each other in search of new ways of understanding life and how organizing activities occur. *A Simpler Way* presents a profoundly different world view that changes how we live our lives and how we can create organizations that thrive.

Hardcover, 168 pages, 9/96 • ISBN 1-881052-95-8 • **Item no. 52958-235 $27.95**

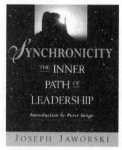

Synchronicity

The Inner Path of Leadership

Joseph Jaworski

S *YNCHRONICITY* is an inspirational guide to developing the most essential leadership capacity for our time: the ability to collectively shape our future. Joseph Jaworski tells the remarkable story of his journey to an understanding of the deep issues of leadership. It is a personal journey that encourages and enlightens all of us wrestling with the profound changes required in public and institutional leadership, and in our individual lives, for the 21st century.

Hardcover, 228 pages, 6/96 • ISBN 1-881052-94-X CIP • **Item no. 5294X-235 $24.95**

Available at your favorite bookstore, or call 1-800-929-2929

Empowerment Takes More than a Minute

Ken Blanchard, John Carlos, and Alan Randolph

EMPOWERMENT TAKES MORE THAN A MINUTE is the book that finally goes beyond the empowerment rhetoric to show managers how to achieve true, lasting results in their organizations. These expert authors explain how to empower the workforce by moving from a command-and-control mindset to a supportive, responsibility-centered environment in which all employees have the opportunity and responsibility to do their best. They explain how to build ownership and trust using three essential keys to making empowerment work in large and small organizations.

Hardcover, 125 pages, 12/96 • ISBN 1-881052-83-4 CIP
Item no. 52834-235 $20.00

Paperback, 125 pages,1/98 • ISBN 1-57675-033-7 **Item no. 50124-235 $12.00**

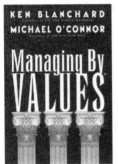

Managing By Values
Ken Blanchard and Michael O'Connor

BASED ON over twenty-five years of research and application, *Managing By Values* provides a practical game plan for defining, clarifying, and communicating an organization's values and insuring that it's practices are in line with those values.

Hardcover, 140 pages, 1/97 • ISBN 1-57675-007-8 CIP
Item no. 50078-235 $20.00

Available at your favorite bookstore, or call 1-800-929-2929